ALMOST GROWN

A New York Memoir

Jesse Malin
with Debra Devi

BROOKLYN, NEW YORK
Publishing books since 1997

All rights reserved. No part of this book may be reproduced, stored in a retrieval system, or transmitted in any form, by any means, including mechanical, electronic, photocopying, recording, or otherwise, without the prior written consent of the publisher.

Published by Akashic Books
©2026 Jesse Malin

ISBN: 978-1-63614-287-6
Library of Congress Control Number: 2025940995
First printing

All photographs courtesy of Jesse Malin unless credited otherwise.
Cover photo courtesy of the Alyssa Taylor Wendt Collection.

EU Authorized Representative details:
Easy Access System Europe
Mustamäe tee 50, 10621 Tallinn, Estonia
gpsr.request@easproject.com

Akashic Books
Brooklyn, New York
Instagram, X, Facebook: AkashicBooks
www.akashicbooks.com
info@akashicbooks.com

For Enid, Paul, Arthur, Renee, and Howie

And to Jak Tollin-DeSalvo

Table of Contents

Prologue: Prisoner of Second Avenue . . . 7
Chapter 1: New Kid . . . 9
Chapter 2: Suicide on Both Sides . . . 15
Chapter 3: Flying Saucers at Goldie's . . . 20
Chapter 4: Stomachache Sundays . . . 28
Chapter 5: 31 Flavors . . . 34
Chapter 6: 7 Train to Glory . . . 43
Chapter 7: Fast Kiss . . . 51
Chapter 8: Last Car on the Line . . . 55
Chapter 9: Making a Scene . . . 64
Chapter 10: Chinese Wops . . . 73
Chapter 11: Mexico City . . . 80
Chapter 12: University of the Streets . . . 89
Chapter 13: Don't Tell Your Sister . . . 97
Chapter 14: Misfits at the Ritz . . . 105
Chapter 15: Keep Your Hands Off of Me . . . 113
Chapter 16: Tao of Love and Sex . . . 120

Chapter 17: Citizen of the World . . . 128
Chapter 18: Young Anarchists (in Love) . . . 136
Chapter 19: The Angels of Van Dam Street . . . 145
Chapter 20: Man with Van . . . 153
Chapter 21: Alphabet Soup . . . 162
Chapter 22: The Green Door . . . 169
Chapter 23: I Got Something for You Boys . . . 178
Chapter 24: Coney Island High . . . 186
Chapter 25: The Hasselhoff . . . 191
Chapter 26: The Garden . . . 199
Chapter 27: The Pirate Ship . . . 204
Chapter 28: Christmas on Fifth . . . 212
Chapter 29: O Sole Mio . . . 221
Chapter 30: The Crown . . . 227
Chapter 31: Spray Paint Heroes . . . 236
Chapter 32: Broken Radio . . . 244
Epilogue: The Father, Son, and the Holy Ghost . . . 252

Prologue

Prisoner of Second Avenue

I started writing this book at the kitchen table in my walk-up apartment in New York City's Lower East Side. I'd come home late at night after a gig and still have energy to burn. So I'd sit scrawling stories and notes onto sheets of paper, and in composition books, into the early morning hours.

I've always been someone who jumps out of bed every morning excited to face the day. I throw up the shades and hit the ground doing push-ups. I love that feeling that anything could happen.

Well, today I'm writing this from a hospital bed. It faces a window that looks out onto Second Avenue and 17th Street. At night, a light shines on a building I've looked at so many times walking these streets. Only now I can't walk. I'm paralyzed from the waist down. The doctors say I've had a spinal stroke. I joke that I'm the Prisoner of Second Avenue.

Six weeks ago, I left my apartment to meet friends for dinner at a favorite spot. We wanted to be together to commemorate the death of my best friend, Howie Pyro, one year before. On the walk over, I felt a strange burning sensation in my hips and lower back.

These are really uncomfortable, I thought, looking down at my old motorcycle boots.

At the restaurant, my legs buckled and I collapsed onto the floor. My buddy Jimmy G. tried to lift me up and help me out the door, so we could get to a hospital.

"Gimme a second," I told him. "I'm gonna shake it off."

Pretty soon, I realized that I wasn't going to shake it off. I couldn't move my legs. Jimmy called for an ambulance. I've been stuck in a hospital bed ever since.

The doctors tell me there's a good chance I'll never walk again. But I am determined to beat this. I am going to walk again, and get back onstage with my band. And walk down the streets of my hometown that I love so much.

There are nights when things feel really dark and scary, and I cry. There are mornings when I feel so helpless that I don't want to open my eyes and face the day, but I do. Physical therapy is grueling, but gives me hope that if I just work hard enough, I will recover my body and the life I had. I've never been afraid to work for what I want.

Throughout this nightmare, I've kept writing. I've always loved telling stories in my songs, usually about other people. But *Almost Grown* is a story I want to tell about myself, the loved ones I've lost, and the beautiful characters I met along the way as I was growing up and coming into my own.

Jesse Malin
NYU Langone Orthopedic Hospital

Chapter 1

New Kid

Throwing things off of the rooftops
Forty buildings all the same
—"Almost Grown"

I've always loved breaking things: toys, windows, bottles, guitars, bands, relationships, tension. I still crack a grin thinking about the time my cousin Matt and I dropped a red plastic *Scooby-Doo* projector—that wasn't even ours!—off the roof of his building in Whitestone, Queens. I was seven; Matt was five. We gleefully watched it tumble through the air, holding our breath until it crashed onto the sidewalk and scattered into shards.

"Fuck yeah!" I screeched.

"Yeah! Fuuuuck!" my cousin screamed. We ran around the roof like Tasmanian devils. Then we charged up and down the stairs a few times for good measure.

The thrill of destruction was always worth the loss of the toy for me. It was such a rush.

Every night when my father came home from work, though, I had to be quiet. He'd arrive grim-faced and uptight after the bus ride in rush-hour traffic from his job in Midtown Manhattan to our apartment. My mother would whisper to me in the kitchen, "Jesse, don't pounce on him. Wait until after he's put his jeans on and had his drink."

My dad had a pair of ripped, faded Levi's dotted with those cloth iron-on patches that were big in the seventies:

Coca-Cola in the familiar white script on a red background; Superman's red *S* on blue; Mickey Mouse. Every weeknight, he changed out of his suit into those jeans and a T-shirt, put on his slippers, and dropped onto my parents' bed. He sat there in silence, leaning against the headboard. My mother would bring him his Jack Daniel's and then retreat to the kitchen.

I kept my distance, peering around the corner as my father slowly shook the ice cubes in his glass, taking the occasional sip, staring into space. It took him a long time to get through that drink. By the time he was nearing the bottom of the glass, I didn't really know what to say to him.

My parents were only twenty-two when I was born in Flushing, Queens in 1967. They hadn't been dating long when they got married and started a family. My sister, Juliet Faith, came along three years later. Our parents loved President John F. Kennedy, so they gave us each the initials J.F. My middle name is Franklin, which has always embarrassed me.

My mother's name was Enid. She had wild curly hair, sparkling brown eyes, and a zany, magnetic energy that drew people to her instantly. She won a "best-looking" trophy while attending the University of Toledo, and dreamed of becoming a singer.

My dad, Paul Malin, was an only child. I remember his parents as dour people with few smiles for anyone. Grandma Sara contracted tuberculosis when my father was two. When she was sent to a Colorado sanatorium for the "mountain-air cure," Grandpa Simon dropped my dad off at a boys home in the Bronx. He didn't hear from either parent again until they picked him up three years later.

My father grew into a tall, darkly handsome guy who loved playing baseball, and dreamed of joining the New York Yankees. He actually played at Yankee Stadium once, but was smart enough to get into Bronx Science, so he went the safer route. He put on a suit and became an accountant.

As an adult, my father asked Grandma Sara why she had never sent him a letter or even a postcard while he was in the boys home.

"You couldn't read," she replied dryly.

Upon meeting my mother for the first time, all my grandparents said to my father was, "She has a chipped tooth." That was how they were, always looking for the flaw.

When I was a teenager, I met Grandpa Simon for lunch at the Capitol Diner in the Bronx. I was wearing blue jeans with a small rip in the left knee.

"Ya got a hole in your jeans," Grandpa Simon noted, staring at it fixedly.

"Yeah, it's really small though," I said, "Who cares? We're just going to the diner."

"Somebody's liable to pass a remark!" he cried, clearly mortified.

It's no wonder my father was self-conscious, wary, and shy. My mother, in contrast, was bubbly and outgoing, like the rest of her family. One time, we were at her parents' house in Long Island for a big party full of boisterous aunts, uncles, cousins, and friends. My dad slipped into a guest room, where he fell asleep.

Later that night, while the party was in full swing, my Aunt Syd opened the door and shouted, "Hey Paul, whaddya do for an encore?" Everybody in the house cracked up.

I think my parents realized pretty early in their marriage that they weren't a great fit. They both loved music; but even that became a source of disagreement. My mother adored the American standards, and sang along to Frank Sinatra and Judy Garland in the car. She loved the Beatles, too. After she was gone, I was surprised to learn that her favorite Beatle was John Lennon. I thought she would have gone for Paul.

My father preferred the rock-and-roll oldies: Elvis, Chuck Berry, Bobby Darin. My dad sang "Heartbreak Hotel" at his bar mitzvah—that's how obsessed he was with Elvis.

Starting at nine a.m. every Sunday morning when I was little, my father turned on the radio and blasted Casey Kasem's entire three-hour *American Top 40 Countdown* of "the biggest songs in the USA!" This drove my mother up the wall. But to my father, the radio charts were like baseball stats, which he liked to memorize. *Which song is number one? How many weeks? What's on the flip side? Who's in the top five with a bullet?*

Casey Kasem always wrapped up his program with the same line: "Keep your feet on the ground and keep reaching for the stars!"

My mother's solution was to buy my father headphones for his birthday. Then she banished him and his radio—rain or shine—to our twenty-second-floor balcony overlooking the traffic-jammed ramp onto the George Washington Bridge.

We moved a lot when I was a kid. From Queens to Fort Lee, then down to South Jersey, where I went to kindergarten, and back to Fort Lee. I was always the new kid, and that, in itself, was rough. Worse, I had a lazy eye and had to wear a big white eye patch over my good eye under my nerdy black horn-rimmed glasses. I hated the sticky feel and plastic smell of that patch. Kids made fun of me, calling me "Four Eyes," "Cyclops," and "One-Eyed Retard."

Every morning, when my mother walked me to the bus stop, I looked up at her pleadingly, as if to say, *Please don't make me go.* She would smile, squeeze my hand, and say, "C'mon, Captain Hook, get on the bus!" She always knew how to give me courage to face the world.

My baby sister was too young for our family's moving

around to bother her—or so we thought. She was a cute little peanut who smiled and giggled, but never said a thing. We only found out she could talk when my mother walked by her room one day and stopped, dumbstruck. Juliet was sitting on her bed holding her teddy bear, chanting, "Get out of Fort Lee. Get out of Fort Lee. Get out of Fort Lee."

The real constant in our young lives was the tension that built up between our parents when my father came home from work, followed by arguing that reverberated through the thin walls of our apartment at night.

Sometimes, though, my folks had company, and I loved that. From my bedroom, I could feel the energy rising, and hear music, laughter, and glasses clinking. It would still be light outside, and I resented being put to bed early with a party going on. It depressed me, even at that age. It felt like death, and I wanted life.

I'd run out into the living room and start dancing and rolling around on the shag carpet. My mother would catch sight of me and scream, "Get back in your room!" I'd last a few minutes before racing out again to dance wildly in front of the hi-fi.

"Fine!" my mother would laugh. She'd hand me a microphone and plug it into the stereo. Oh my God, I loved the sound of my voice so big and warm through the speakers. I'd sing a few lines of Gene Vincent's "Be-Bop-a-Lula" over and over, and feel so powerful. The adults would laugh and applaud, and my dad would yell, "That's enough! Go back to your room!"

Then, suddenly, one night when we didn't have company, my dad flipped out. He and my mother were screaming at each other in the kitchen. I ran out in my pajamas just as he ripped the phone off the wall while she was trying to call her parents. He bolted into the living room, grabbed our bust of

John F. Kennedy, and threw it—*BAM!*—against the wall. It cracked the plaster and thudded to the floor, barely damaged except for a chip off Kennedy's perfect Irish nose.

Wow! I was so excited. Finally, something was happening in this house. Some action, like on *Batman*. Part of me wondered why I wasn't upset or scared, but I shoved that part away.

"We gotta get outta here!" my mother yelled. I dashed into my bedroom and ran back out clutching my plastic gorilla bank full of nickels and pennies. If we were going to leave, we were going to need some money.

Chapter 2

Suicide on Both Sides

*They say the best of comedians
Often battle with depression*
—"Bar Life"

I don't blame all the fighting on my father. My mother was riding her own emotional roller coaster, especially after I was born, when she fell into a severe postpartum depression.

I'm not a big guy, around a hundred and fifty pounds, but I was a nine-pound baby—and when my mother was in labor with me, it wasn't going well. The doctors performed an emergency C-section, ripping her open. Back then, doctors didn't know that a woman's hormones can crash after a C-section. For some new mothers, this can be disastrous.

When the nurse brought me to her, my mother flipped out because I was wrapped in a pink blanket, instead of blue for boys. By the time my father took us home, her rage had dissipated, but she was nearly comatose with depression. My mother's parents stepped in to help care for me, especially my grandfather, Papa Artie.

My grandparents eventually dragged my mother out of bed and to the shrink they swore was *the best!*—Dr. Rutsky in Long Island. My father thought this guy was a nut. For starters, he had "accidentally" shot his wife in the foot. But whenever my mother's parents really dug something—whether it was their favorite Chinese restaurant or a gun-toting therapist—they were always convinced it was *the best!* And there was no arguing with them.

Their concern for my mother was not unwarranted. Her grandfather, Jozef Rutkowsky, slit his throat in the bathroom when he was fifty-five.

Papa Joe was eighteen when he arrived in New York from Kiev in 1913. He became a junk collector, driving his horse-drawn cart along First Avenue from downtown all the way up to East Harlem, shouting, "Junkman! Junkman!" People came out of their tenements with rusty bikes, old clothes, chipped dishes, bald tires. He took their junk home to the Lower East Side to fix up and resell.

The family rumor was that Papa Joe killed himself in 1950 because he was depressed about being out of work and unable to provide for his family. Even though he was struggling, my mother told me that when she was a little girl and Papa Joe came to visit, he always slid a few dollars in between the couch cushions for her and her brother to find after he left.

I think of Papa Joe sometimes when I'm walking around the Lower East Side. It's funny that this old ghetto my relatives worked so hard to get out of is where I found the music, and made my bones.

Dr. Rutsky's prescription for my mother's depression was to put her on heavy doses of Valium, and relentlessly cajole her into having another baby. She just needed to "get back on the horse," he said.

My father thought this was insane, so Dr. Rutsky insisted that he come for a session. My dad knew he wouldn't have a moment's peace until he went. Dr. Rutsky diagnosed him with anxiety, and prescribed massive doses of Valium for him, too.

Granted, my dad was an anxious guy. Any little thing

made him break out in a cold sweat. When I was a kid, he used to send me running for a towel whenever something—or someone—was sending him over the edge. I ran for a lot of towels.

Pretty soon Dr. Rutsky had my father so whacked out on Valium that "I didn't know whether I was coming or going," he told me later. He caved in to the pressure to have another child, and Juliet was born in 1970 via C-section. My mother experienced another debilitating bout of postpartum depression.

I don't remember much of this, of course. I remember my mother as wickedly funny, kooky, and adventurous. If she couldn't afford tickets to take my sister to a show at Radio City Music Hall, she'd pull her hat down dramatically over her face and they'd walk in backwards together. "By hook or by crook," she'd say; we would always find a way to get by and make things happen.

Even though we were Jewish, my mother's side of the family loved to celebrate Christmas. Juliet and I believed wholeheartedly in Santa when we were little. I'd get so excited that I would try to go to bed as early as possible on Christmas Eve, so that Christmas morning would arrive sooner.

My mother was loving and indulgent, but also tough. If I said "the F word," or even just "Shut up," she'd point at the kitchen and bark, "Step into my office, young man." She'd squirt liquid Ivory dish soap onto a wooden spoon and shove it in my mouth, yelling, "Swallow it! Swallow it!"

Suicidal tendencies ran in my father's family, too. Grandpa Simon was over six feet tall and around two hundred pounds, with thinning hair and distant brown eyes. He claimed to have faked a nervous breakdown while in the army to avoid fighting in World War II—but rumor had it his breakdown might have been real. Whenever we visited, he paced around his apartment like a caged animal, running his tongue over his missing front teeth with his lips closed, barely saying a word to me or Juliet.

Grandpa Simon had been a cop at the notorious 41st Precinct in the South Bronx known as "Fort Apache." At night, he moonlighted lugging jukeboxes and coin-operated pool tables out of the back of his station wagon into bars and nightclubs in Harlem and the Bronx. He stocked the jukeboxes with vinyl 45s—from doo-wop and James Brown to Hector Rivera, Joe Cuba, the Supremes, and Dion.

After retiring from the NYPD, Grandpa Simon became a grade-school teacher in a Latino neighborhood. He still spent nights and Saturdays dragging around jukeboxes and pool tables. He also sold the colorful plastic flags that bodegas used to announce grand openings. He was probably the only teacher the kids saw in their neighborhood after school—balancing on a rickety ladder on some uneven Bronx street, tacking up those flags.

Between class periods, Grandpa Simon would slip into a bathroom stall and take a nap on the toilet. On Sundays, my dad told me, he would lie in the bathtub all day long, not saying a word.

Grandpa Simon worked like a dog because he was forever convinced he was about to "go under." He developed a hernia the size of an orange that bulged out of his side. He showed it to me once when I was little.

"Grandpa!" I cried, "What is that thing?"

"It's a hernia."

"What's that?"

"Ya get it from lifting heavy things."

"Then shouldn't you stop lifting them, Grandpa?"

"Nah, ya just push it back in and keep working," he grunted. "Like this, see?"

I almost fainted.

As I got older, Grandpa Simon got nuttier. After a minor car accident, he became convinced that he was going to be sued and lose everything. His paranoia grew until one day he climbed onto the kitchen table and jumped out the window of his apartment on Kappock Street.

The flaw in his plan to end it all was that he and Grandma Sara lived on the second floor. Grandpa Simon landed on the driveway—busted up, with both ankles broken, but not dead.

Grandma Sara's sister, Aunt Ann, lived on the eighth floor. My mother used to joke, "If he wanted to do it right, he shoulda gone up to Aunt Ann's apartment!"

Chapter 3

Flying Saucers at Goldie's

My grandfather worked these streets
Took my grandmother to the Roseland beat
   —"Burning the Bowery"

Grandpa Simon wound up in the mental ward at the VA hospital, getting shock treatment for depression. When we went to visit, he looked like a skeleton—all nose and bones, no teeth, twitching in a terry-cloth robe. He eventually regained some weight and moved into a nursing home, where I visited him a few times a year until he passed away when I was twelve.

I often wonder if this vein of depression and anxiety running through both sides of my family was a curse that these Eastern European Jews carried over from the Old World. After all, it had been trying to wipe them out for centuries.

My buffer from all this insanity was my mother's kind and loving father, Papa Artie. He was a handsome guy who looked a bit like Gregory Peck, with high cheekbones, thick dark hair, and strong brows. Papa was in great shape and looked very young for his age. He loved to jump out of bed and do his push-ups and jumping jacks first thing in the morning. He was always singing, humming a tune, or telling funny little jokes. He seemed truly happy to be alive.

I believe his sunny disposition was a choice. I say this because Papa Artie grew up poor on the Lower East Side during the Great Depression. His mother died shortly after he was born, and when his father slit his throat in the bathroom, Papa was just thirty-two.

Once in a blue moon, I would catch him sitting silently in his recliner, steeped in a quiet sadness. But when he saw me, he would cover it with a smile. He showed me that happiness is a choice, and a little kindness goes a long way. He was constantly saving lost dogs or injured birds; and giving rides to hitchhikers and soldiers, or money to unhoused people on the streets.

Papa had a small business called Toddle Time, visiting families around Queens to photograph their children. He was wonderful with me and Juliet, and made every day feel like a super-fun adventure. He and my mother taught me how to swim at Rockaway Beach. We'd put on our flippers and swim out as far as we could. My mother had a daredevil streak. She'd push her luck, swimming out so far that the lifeguards would stand up and scream at her to get back. That used to scare me. But maybe that's where I got my own daredevil traits.

Once, Papa and I drove out to those three sandy miles along the bottom edge of Brooklyn known as Coney Island. Papa told me that when he was young, Coney was the place to be. Everybody hung out all summer at the most famous beach and amusement park in the world.

But the 1970s were hard on New York, and even harder on Coney. It had fallen into a sorry state. The Parachute Jump was closed and the Cyclone roller coaster was being threatened with demolition. The place was so empty and creepy that as we walked around, I was scared something terrible might happen to us.

Papa and I rode around on the go-carts a few times, but then we quickly got back in the car. Still, I could almost see the ghosts of laughing teenagers, and feel the excitement and romance of what once was.

* * *

As a young man, Papa Artie worked for a liquor distributor, selling booze to all the bars up and down the Bowery. One day, he suggested to his boss that they slap custom labels on the bottles so that Joe's Bar, for example, could boast its own "brand" of gin.

His boss thought that was a great idea. The labels were a big success, until a guy was cracked in the head with a bottle during a bar fight up in Harlem, and died. Thanks to the label, the police traced the murder weapon back to a Bowery dive.

And that was the end of that.

Years later, when I was living on the Lower East Side, Papa came to visit me and we went for a walk. He told me that when he was a kid, he and his friends would jump in the East River on a hot summer day and float on their backs, letting the current carry them uptown. They'd climb out and catch the trolley back downtown.

As Papa and I walked down First Avenue, he pointed to a row of six-story brick tenements from the 1800s.

"These buildings will still be here in another hundred years," he declared passionately.

He was right. I've seen this neighborhood go through all kinds of changes, and those tenements are still hanging in there.

We walked over to where Papa's high school once stood, on the corner of 9th Street and Stuyvesant. Hebrew Tech was a vocational school for the children of the Jewish refugees flooding into the Lower East Side. Papa told me that Albert Einstein once came to speak there, fresh off the boat.

"A great scientist is going to speak to you today," Papa Artie's teacher had announced when introducing Einstein. "He just arrived from Germany, and he taught himself English on the boat ride over."

Einstein spoke briefly to the class, asking about their studies, and telling them a little bit about his own work. After he left, the teacher said, "Do you realize that what that man just said in a few sentences would take pages of mathematics to explain?"

Einstein was very nice, Papa said. "And he was Jewish!"

That was a refrain I heard from Papa a lot as a kid. He liked to take me on walks when my family visited him and Grandma Renee in Long Island, and point out successful Jewish men.

"See that guy over there, Jesse?" Papa would say. "Look at him. Handsome. Strong. Look at his nice car. He's a doctor. He's got money, a beautiful wife." Then Papa would lean in and softly whisper, like he was telling me a secret, "He's Jewish."

Or he might nudge me and say, "Look at that guy. He's so tough—full of muscles. He used to be a boxer. Such a powerhouse! He owns that gas station. He makes lots of money." Then, in a whisper, "He's Jewish."

After his father committed suicide, Papa started going to temple regularly. He took me sometimes, but I couldn't understand anything the rabbi was saying in Hebrew through his beard.

Being a Jew meant a lot to my grandfather, and he wanted me to embrace it, too. Yet he also understood the risks of being Jewish. He had lived through World War II, and experienced a lot of anti-Semitism when he served in the US military. He had changed his last name from Rutkowsky to Ross. Maybe that was why he whispered.

After my father ripped the phone off our kitchen wall, my mother fled with me and Juliet to her parents' house in North Woodmere. I was delighted to be out of Fort Lee and staying with Papa Artie and Grandma Renee. For me, their home was a place of fun and safety.

I loved waking up on Saturday mornings to the sound of Grandma Renee bustling into the kitchen with brown paper bags from her weekly supermarket trip. I knew she had bought all my favorites. I found comfort in knowing there was plenty of food in the house, which wasn't always the case in our apartment.

Papa loved watching his favorite movies over and over again, like I do today. After dinner, we'd catch classics like *The Four Feathers*, *Mister Roberts*, or *High Noon*. And, of course, if any of the stars were Jewish, he'd be quick to let me know.

After watching our movie, we'd go stand on the back porch and stare up into the darkness. Papa would smoke his pipe, which smelled good and sweet, and show me Polaris—the North Star—and the Big Dipper. He had been a navigator in the US Air Force, and knew all the constellations.

My grandparents had separate bedrooms, so I slept in Papa Artie's room. I got scared in the dark one time and whispered, "It's such a long night, Papa. It's such a looong night."

"Go to sleep, Jesse," he whispered back, "'Cause in the morning we're gonna make a brand-new cereal, Gooky Cookies!"

I was a fanatic for the sugar-loaded cereals of the time—Count Chocula, Franken Berry, Cap'n Crunch, Froot Loops—and the cheap prizes I dug out of the bottoms of their boxes. I was such a hyperactive kid that all the sugar was like giving speed to a monkey. This promise of an exciting new cereal was enough to get me to settle down.

Sure enough, in the morning Papa bustled around the kitchen breaking chocolate chip cookies into our bowls.

He covered them with grape jelly and poured milk over the whole concoction, shouting, "Gooky Cookies!" It was kind of awful, but Juliet and I loved it.

After breakfast, I'd trail him to the garage, where he'd take his folding bike out of the trunk of his old Buick. I'd climb onto the metal rack in the back, and we'd pedal to the candy store to get his *New York Times* and some candy and toys for me.

We'd take our loot to the backyard, and Papa would be almost as thrilled as I was to fire off our rubber-band Whirly Birds and water-powered rockets, and run after them. A lot of them got stuck on the roof, but we didn't care. After all that excitement, Papa would sit in his lawn chair in the sun and read the *Times*. I was fascinated by how huge the paper was—bigger than I was. Papa showed me how to fold and read it properly. To this day, the smell of ink on a fresh *New York Times* still reminds me of him.

Grandma Renee was a sweet lady, but I could tell she didn't like Papa relaxing in the backyard. She'd come to the screen door in a huff, rolling her eyes. I didn't understand why that made her so cranky.

Later, I learned she didn't think Papa worked hard enough. She was mad that she had to get a job in Manhattan to help cover the mortgage—even though moving out of Queens had been her idea.

When she and Papa Artie got married, they followed Papa's family—and lots of their friends—from the Lower East Side to a close-knit Queens neighborhood called Middle Village. My grandparents loved living there, near a big park where there were lots of parties all the time.

But when my mother was in grade school, she hit that awkward age when you look kind of funny because you're still growing into who you'll become. She wasn't the beauty yet that she would become—and some mean girls began tormenting her. They made fun of her name, Enid, calling her "Eat It" and "Penis." Instead of helping my mother face down her bullies, Grandma Renee insisted on moving to Long Island to get away from them. Papa Artie never really got over leaving Queens.

He and Grandma Renee still saw their old friends, though. Like my mother, Grandma Renee had a big, beautiful voice. After a few drinks at a party or wedding, she didn't need much encouragement to jump up and sing her favorite number, "A Hundred Years from Today." The entire gang would drive out to Gibson, Long Island on a Saturday night to whoop it up at Goldie's Restaurant—an Italian place that, of course, was *the best!*

I was seven, and still believed in Santa Claus. Despite Papa's best efforts to get me into Judaism, I had also developed a secret fascination with Jesus. He looked like a rock star with his lean body, long hair, and crown of thorns.

I learned in temple that the Jews were still waiting for their savior. That seemed kinda weird to me. Waiting and waiting for thousands of years. Christians had their guy already. He was right there, hanging from a cross in front of their eyes every Sunday, bleeding and sacrificing himself like a hero.

Why would God tell the Christians one thing and the Jews something else? That didn't make sense to me. How could the Jews be the Chosen People? Did that mean God didn't like anybody else?

Then I found out that Jesus was a Jew. Now I was totally confused. I wasn't sure I could believe in God. Santa Claus? Yeah. God? Maybe.

Papa Artie took the family to Goldie's for dinner one Saturday night. Red-velvet clown paintings adorned the walls, and a band in the corner was playing "Sweet Caroline" by Neil Diamond. I was clutching a toy gun that shot a plastic flying saucer into the air really fast.

"Jess, please don't shoot that gun off in the restaurant," Papa said. I obediently shoved it into my pocket. While we were waiting in the crowded bar, Papa walked into the dining room to scout for a table.

I took out my gun and shot it off—ZOOM!

Papa Artie came trotting back into the bar, holding a napkin to his bloody nose. "Jess!" he cried, shaking an incriminating plastic flying saucer at me. "I told you not to shoot that thing off in here!"

Wow, I thought, *there is a God! And here he is, punishing me for being bad. How else, out of all those people packed into Goldie's, did I manage to hit Papa right in the nose?* I felt like the worst kid on the planet.

Papa Artie put his arm around me and gave me a squeeze. I knew he forgave me and everything was going to be all right. Plus, the existence of God was no longer in question—at least for the time being.

Chapter 4

Stomachache Sundays

Messed up like the father, who couldn't see the son
Messed up like the outlaw, who blamed it on the gun
            —"Cigarettes and Violets"

After a few weeks at my grandparents' house, my mother moved with me and Juliet to a one-bedroom apartment in a six-story redbrick building in Whitestone, Queens. Juliet and I shared the bedroom; my mother slept on the pull-out couch in the living room.

That's when I knew my father wasn't coming back. He was living in a high-rise in Manhattan on 60th Street and Third Avenue with three other divorced guys from his job. Juliet and I were to see him on weekends.

My mother got a job at the Bloomingdale's makeup counter in the city. At night, she waitressed, or sang wherever she could get a gig—like the struggling single mom in her favorite movie, *Alice Doesn't Live Here Anymore*.

On Saturdays, or sometimes just on Sundays, my father picked us up in his used Cadillac. That thing was like driving a living room down the street. There was always a woman in the front seat with long hair and big sunglasses. She would last for maybe a week or two, and then there'd be a new one. My dad traded in his car a lot, too, always looking for the upgrade.

He drove into Manhattan, heading up the Bowery to avoid traffic and save on tolls. New York City was a total wreck in the mid-1970s, especially downtown. Drunks were sprawled all over the sidewalks along the Bowery. Juliet would stare out the window wide-eyed.

"Daddy, why are all those guys lying on the sidewalk?" she once asked.

"They drank too many sodas," he replied dryly.

At red lights, bums tottered toward our car and dragged filthy rags or squeegees across the windshield, smearing it with God knows what. My father would flip out, screaming, "Get the fuck outta here!" in his heavy Bronx accent, frantically pounding his horn. Even Juliet knew: you don't touch the car!

I walked into our bedroom one afternoon, and Juliet was banging on the steering wheel of a little toy car she'd gotten for her birthday, cursing like a sailor in her sweet-little-girl voice: "Sonna ya bitch! Sonna ya bitch bastard!" She thought that was how you drove.

My father didn't talk much on those car rides—to us or his girlfriends—but he played music on the eight-track player—Chuck Berry, Elton John, Jim Croce—that would influence me for the rest of my life.

I first heard "Bad, Bad Leroy Brown" cruising up Third Avenue with my dad. Leroy Brown was such a badass, *"meaner than a junkyard dog"*! That song was an action movie—with a big shootout at the end—wrapped up in three thrilling, piano-pounding minutes. And Croce's "I Got a Name" still makes me cry to this day.

I've got a name, I've got a name
And I carry it with me like my daddy did
But I'm livin' the dream that he kept hid

I felt like my father was speaking to me through these songs.

His new place was a cross between a frat house and Spencer Gifts, decorated with black lights, lava lamps, and posters of Groucho Marx, W.C. Fields, and Marilyn Monroe tacked to the walls. So were Polaroids of him and his roommates smashing lemon meringue pies into each other's faces on some beach, and a Playmate of the Month calendar. A glass coffee table was strewn with *National Lampoon* magazines, a deck of naked-lady cards, and a gag set of plastic teeth that I would wind up and send chattering across the tabletop over and over while Juliet and I sat around on the couch.

My dad didn't talk a whole lot at his apartment, either. Mostly, Juliet and I looked at magazines or the *New York Times*, and watched TV. When no one was looking, I rifled through the *Playboy*s stacked on a living-room end table.

Once, Juliet was rummaging through the nightstand drawer in my father's bedroom and pulled out a pink torpedo-shaped vibrator. "What's this, Daddy?" she asked.

"Oh, it's for massages," he replied. He turned it on and touched it to her back as it buzzed. "See?"

Dinner was usually McDonald's or pizza. After dinner I listened to FM radio stations on the puffy headphones in my father's bedroom.

The Beekman Theatre was around the corner, with long lines of people waiting to be let in to the weekend shows. I liked to walk over there with him to see what was playing. *The Yakuza, Death Wish, The Exorcist*. Those titles thrilled me. So did the sounds of the city: sirens wailing, cars honking, screams, laughter, and, in the summer, the Mister Softee truck playing that haunting song over and over again.

Back at the apartment, I dug out the *Times* Arts and Leisure section and studied the full-page movie ads to figure out which one I should pester my father to take me to see. I was looking for action. I'd heard *Taxi Driver* was the most violent film ever made. But the ad in the *Times* was just some guy standing in front of a taxicab, not a cool killer with a cool gun like James Bond or Charles Bronson. It looked like any old night in New York City to me.

Seeing a movie together gave my dad and me something to talk about. Once, one of his girlfriends complained, "All you two talk about is movies or music. Don't you ever talk about anything *real*?" That made me feel bad, but my dad grinned at me, raising an eyebrow. It was nice, for that moment, to feel like we were in cahoots.

One weekend, my father might be happy to take us to the movies. But the next weekend, he might snap, "What, am I made of money? I always have to entertain you kids? We can't just sit here and talk?"

Many weekends, he didn't come for me and Juliet at all.

Maybe my father's tense, unpredictable nature is why I was drawn to movies and TV shows starring explosive, violent heroes. I kept trying to understand what made my father tick—and how to avoid setting him off like a time bomb.

Or maybe I was trying to understand how men were supposed to act. I was fascinated by the hero who was pushed to the edge and exploded with swift, righteous rage—like Billy Jack.

When you need him, he's always there! the *Billy Jack* movie poster declared. He was a Navajo outlaw martial-arts master who defended women, children, people of color—anyone being abused or exploited. When Billy Jack delivered a roundhouse kick to some bastard's head, the audience cheered. You knew the guy deserved it, and that felt so good.

I was constantly getting into fights at school, so maybe I was just trying to understand what made *me* tick. My feelings were a jumbled-up mystery to me. All I knew was I felt like an outsider—different from everybody else—and I had a short fuse. I was embarrassed that I was sharing a bedroom with my sister and that our mother slept on the couch. I didn't want anyone to come over and notice that we only had a small black-and-white TV, and no stereo anymore.

It didn't help that our parents openly bitched about each other to me and Juliet.

"Your dad doesn't give us enough money to pay even a quarter of the rent! He gives us nothing!" my mother would shout.

"Look how she's raising you, like wild animals!" my father yelled. "Your mother and her crazy dreams! Your mother and that crazy family!"

Being caught in between them made me scared and confused, and Juliet silent.

Juliet was very shy, but she was really sweet. In later years, I sometimes teased and taunted her. I don't know why; maybe because I was angry and didn't know how to handle it. But in those early years, we were pretty tight.

Her baby teeth were falling out and she couldn't say my name right. Whenever a relative gave her a little gift, or maybe a five-dollar bill, she would softly call out, "Chess, Chess!" and hand it up to me. That's just how Juliet was.

One evening, I was flipping through the ten channels on our TV when I noticed this cool Black family hanging out together in a funky apartment that looked a lot like mine. They were hilarious, so I stuck around to watch my first episode of *Good Times*.

The father, James, worked two jobs to make ends meet, just like my mother. The oldest son, J.J. Walker—"Kid Dyn-o-Mite!"—was a crazy artist who crashed on the pull-out couch in the living room. J.J. dreamed of making it big one day and moving his family to a better place. So did my mother.

Good Times made me laugh. But what I loved was how the Evans family joked around about being poor, and always made the best of it. They never let it get them down. *Good Times* became my favorite TV show. It helped me shed some of the embarrassment I had been hauling around for too long.

When Juliet and I did visit my father, and he drove us home on a Sunday evening, he always tuned in to *The Doo-Wop Shop* on the oldies radio station. Those haunting songs from the 1950s with their ghostly harmonies spooked the hell out of me on our twilight ride.

The stores were all closed. The streets were dead. There was nothing to distract me from the anxious, guilty feeling that would start to creep in. I hadn't finished my homework. I knew I was going to be in trouble at school on Monday morning. That was the beginning of my stomachache Sundays.

If there was traffic, forget it, my father was going to lose it.

"God damn it, this fucking bridge!" he would screech, pounding the steering wheel as his voice climbed several octaves.

My stomach would start to hurt. It got worse as he turned down our street, because I knew how upset he was going to get searching for a parking spot. He usually got fed up, and dropped us off in front of our building.

Our block was dark at night, with few streetlights. Often, my mother wasn't home yet from her waitressing job, or a date. I hated the lonely feeling of opening the door and ushering my sister into the dark while I fumbled for the light switch.

That bad Sunday feeling has stuck with me. Sometimes I'll be on tour and have a day off in some nowhere town. If it's dead quiet, with nobody around, my stomach will start to hurt, and then I'll realize, *Oh . . . it's Sunday.*

Chapter 5

31 Flavors

*You started out with nothing but lonely days
You used to like the sad songs of doom and gloom*
—"Brooklyn"

Elton John was my gateway drug.

"Crocodile Rock" was the first single I ever owned. My cousin Matt and I wore it out on my plastic record player. We'd play it really loud, and jump up and down on my single bed, trying to hit the ceiling. That's how we knew a song was good—if it made us go crazy.

"I'm Henry VIII, I Am" by Herman's Hermits was another bed-jumper—fast and brash. We loved shouting, "*Second verse, same as the first!*"

Rock and roll was everywhere. "The Loco-Motion" by Grand Funk Railroad blasting from the jukebox at Freddie's Pizza. Zeppelin's "Black Dog" screaming out of a radio on the bus. "Brother Louie" by Stories deafening me and Juliet on the Himalaya ride at Adventurer's Inn. Stoners in green army jackets and floppy suede hats rocking Lynyrd Skynyrd and the Grateful Dead in the schoolyard at night.

I couldn't wait to be old enough to go to a rock concert. Whenever the lights went down in my school auditorium for some boring assembly, I imagined we were about to see a real loud band come out and blow the roof off the place.

My growing passion for rock and roll took the edge off the hurt and confusion I was reeling from after my parents' divorce. My father came around even less often to pick up Juliet and me on the weekend. Sometimes I stood on our stoop waiting for hours, but he didn't show.

Matt's parents were divorced, too. He and his mother lived across the street. Matt's father was Uncle Jon, my mom's younger brother. He arrived like clockwork every Saturday to pick up Matt and take him to amusement parks, James Bond movies, and pizza places.

Sometimes, Uncle Jon saw me waiting outside and invited me to come along. Maybe he felt bad for me—I don't know. We always had the best time. I never felt like I was walking on eggshells, the way I did with my father. Uncle Jon always knew the best pizza places. Pizza would be my electric chair meal. Even when it's bad, it's good.

Other times, I stood outside hoping Uncle Jon might invite me along, but he and Matt just waved hello and went on their way. I felt lost, even though I sort of understood that Uncle Jon wanted some time alone with his son.

Maybe that's why "Crocodile Rock" hooked me. The loneliness swirling beneath it pulled me in.

But the years went by and the rock just died
Susie went and left us for some foreign guy

People left in Elton John's songs. They split up in "Love Lies Bleeding," or bailed with some foreign guy. My father had left and now it loomed over me that sometimes people leave, and there is nothing you can do about it.

Every morning, my mother took a bus and the subway to her job at Bloomingdale's in Midtown Manhattan. One day, she told me, Elvis Presley walked right past her makeup counter—wearing a veil.

I loved it when my mother took me to work with her. I met her fun gay friends who were makeup artists on the floor. She let me wander around the neighborhood—warning me not to go too far—and gave me fifty cents to ride the brand-new Roosevelt Island Tram, way up high over the East River.

I felt so excited navigating the chaotic, crowded sidewalks by myself. People were shouting in different languages and dodging each other. They'd step right over some guy passed out on the sidewalk, or drop a few coins into a panhandler's cup, without missing a beat. They might slow down to grab a "dirty water dog" from a street cart and eat it on the run. As I hustled along, I smelled sauerkraut, burnt pretzels, and sweet roasted nuts—cut with BO and piss.

Midtown was much cooler back then. I rode the escalators inside Alexander's department store, and ventured into Jumpin' Jack Flash, drawn by the outrageous platform boots in the window. That store carried everything a rock star or a groupie could want—from embroidered velvet suits and sexy miniskirts to sharp, snakeskin boots.

I fell in love with Manhattan on those walks. It's been a lifelong romance ever since.

My mother also tried to make money as a singer, landing the occasional nightclub gig. When she was out late with friends, or at a gig, Juliet and I stayed home with our babysitters, which I didn't mind at all. They were the coolest girls I had ever met in their tube tops, bell bottoms, platform sandals, Farrah Fawcett hair, and feather earrings. I thought they were all so wild and sexy. I fantasized that one of them might come on to me, like in a movie I'd watched on TV called *Summer of '42*.

I grilled them about movies and bands. They loved Led Zeppelin, the Who, and Elton John the most. I obsessed over their issues of *Cream* and *Circus*, staring at the photos. I noticed that Roger Daltrey and Ozzy Osbourne wore big crosses around their necks.

"Are there any Jewish rock stars?" I asked my favorite babysitter, Celeste.

"Um . . . Bob Dylan?" she said.

I found a picture of Dylan with a little acoustic guitar, wearing strange white makeup and a hat with flowers in it. He had curly hair like mine. I didn't think he looked very rock and roll.

I was already on the fence about Judaism. Thinking that there were no cool Jewish rock stars pushed me over it. I quit Hebrew school, and I never had a bar mitzvah—which broke Papa Artie's heart.

Growing up in Queens, I had no idea that Jews were a minority. Today, I'm still not religious, but I'm Jewish for toasted bagels, Mel Brooks, Lenny Bruce, cold beet borscht, and Lou Reed. I'm Jewish because of Hitler and the Holocaust. And if somebody makes an anti-Semitic crack in a bar, I'm even more Jewish.

I still don't buy into the Chosen People part, though. We all should have a place in this world.

Celeste gave me her copy of *Goodbye Yellow Brick Road*. I pored over the lyrics and drawings strewn across the album's triple-gatefold cover. It was like a road map to the grown-up world.

I stared at the photos of Elton and his band. The drummer looked like a pretty girl with his long brown hair. That fascinated me—a guy who kind of looked like a girl. I'd never seen that before.

I was so captivated by the empathy in Elton's voice on "Candle in the Wind." It made me cry. Something terrible had happened to this Marilyn Monroe—but what? I studied the words curving gently around her beautiful face, trying to figure it out. *"And I would've liked to have known you, but I was just a kid . . ."*

Elton was a stocky guy with thinning hair—an unlikely rock star. Like me, he wore glasses. But instead of being ashamed, Elton flaunted the biggest, craziest glasses in the world. He was small, like me, so he wore giant, silver platform boots emblazoned with his initials. Elton showed me that if you feel insecure about something, turn it up! So big that no one can touch you.

That summer, I went to a crappy YMCA camp off Northern Boulevard in Flushing. The "recreation area" was a fenced-off concrete courtyard lined with weeds—and full of bees. Kids got stung all the time, so there was constant screaming and crying.

I was swatting away a pesky wasp one day when a ten-year-old boy came up to me. "My friend had me suck his dick for two dollars last night," he announced. "Ya want me to suck your dick?"

I was totally confused. Why would he want to get pee pee in his mouth? And why would I give him money to put my dick in his mouth and suck on it? Wouldn't that hurt? "Uh, no thanks," I mumbled.

"That's cool," he shrugged, and walked off.

In 1976, Elton John came out as bisexual. He was my hero, and kids at school were calling him a faggot and saying he liked to suck dick. Maybe that was something fun, after all. I figured if Elton liked men, that was fine by me.

That was a good message for me to get, growing up in queer-hating Queens.

When *Dog Day Afternoon* came to the Quartet theater in my neighborhood, Papa Artie took me to see it. Al Pacino was very hot at the time—especially out in the boroughs—thanks to *Serpico* and *The Godfather*.

Pacino played a real guy named John Wojtowicz—"Sonny Wortzik" in *Dog Day Afternoon*—who tried to rob a Brooklyn bank. Inflation was out of control and jobs were scarce. People were broke and fed up. In our packed theater, everybody cheered for Sonny as he nervously held up the bank.

Midway through the film, we found out that Sonny needs the money to pay for his trans lover's surgery. Not a single person yelled "Faggot!" or got up and walked out. Pacino's performance was so gripping that we all rooted for him to the bitter end. It wasn't about being gay or straight; it was about what you might do for love when you're really desperate.

For my birthday, my mother took me and four friends to see the movie I had been pestering her about for months: *One Flew Over the Cuckoo's Nest*. She let me get my way a lot when I was a kid. She told me once it was because she felt guilty about the depression she fell into when I was born.

As young as we were, my friends and I loved that movie. I related strongly to Jack Nicholson's character, R.P. McMurphy. He was a clown, a fighter, and an outcast.

Afterward, my mom took us to Baskin-Robbins 31 Flavors for ice cream. I got my favorite, pink bubblegum, laced with frozen chunks of gum that could break your teeth.

The good thing about my obsession with movies was that it got me into books. I started reading *One Flew Over the Cuckoo's Nest* by Ken Kesey right after seeing the movie.

One Monday, my teacher announced that Friday would be "Book Day." We were to come to the school auditorium dressed as a character from our favorite book. I was so excited. I worked on my costume all week. I took a deck of cards and cut pictures of naked ladies out of a *Playboy* I found. I carefully stapled one to every card in the deck.

On Book Day, I put on jeans and a white T-shirt, and laced up my work boots. I stuffed my frizzy brown hair under a black knit cap and pulled it down low over my forehead. I tucked my porno card deck into my T-shirt sleeve, just like McMurphy in the movie.

When it was my turn to get onstage and speak into the microphone, I proudly declared, "I'm Randle Patrick McMurphy from *One Flew Over the Cuckoo's Nest!*" Nobody applauded. Teachers snickered and rolled their eyes in the front row.

That landed me in a therapist's office. My teacher told my mother she was concerned that I wasn't experiencing a childhood, because I was excessively interested in violent movies and dirty magazines.

Actually, I just thought kids' stuff was stupid. I wanted to hang out with teenagers and grown-ups. That seemed a lot more fun to me.

By now, I had discovered the TV show *Happy Days* and I had a new hero—the Fonz. I became obsessed with the 1950s. I put Vaseline in my hair and greased it back with a pocket comb. I was desperate to get my hands on a black leather motorcycle jacket. My father finally bought me a cheap vinyl knockoff at Korvette's. It still looked pretty cool with the collar flipped up.

When my dad handed it to me, he said, "You can have this because I wasn't allowed to have one when I was your age."

That made me feel close to him, for a minute.

My mother sent me to a shrink named Dr. Feldinger, who wore a three-piece suit. At our first session, he had me get down on the floor with him to pitch pennies. I guess he was trying to bring out the child in me. All I thought was: *What the hell is this?* He was old, though, so I figured he could tell me what it was like in the fifties.

First, though, I peppered Dr. Feldinger with questions about some movies. I was trying to figure out if they were worth hounding my parents to take me to see them. "Why is that Clint Eastwood movie called *Dirty Harry*?" I asked. I wanted to know if it had naked ladies in it.

"Well," Dr. Feldinger replied, "because he hits below the belt."

I had no idea what that meant. "Tell me about the fifties!" I said. "What was it like?"

"Well," Dr. Feldinger replied, "I grew up in the forties."

This guy's a square, I thought.

My mother pulled the plug on therapy after a few weeks. That was fine by me, since Dr. Feldinger wasn't going to tell me about the fifties. Besides, I had a new obsession.

One night, Juliet and I were watching *The Paul Lynde Halloween Special*. I was feeling restless and bored. Suddenly, flaming torches lit up around the stage, a fire alarm blared, and white smoke poured across our TV screen. Out ran four larger-than-life monsters in crazy makeup, black leather, and silver studs—ready to eat up the whole world. They were the wildest things I had ever seen.

Smoke bombs exploded with every chord Ace Frehley banged on his guitar. Peter Criss pounded the drums for "Detroit Rock City" while Gene Simmons prowled the stage with his black bass. KISS was loud, tough, scary, bloody— in your face! These guys were pure power—jumping around with everything I wanted to scream at the world. They were singing to kids like me who were lost, frustrated, and needed something exciting to live for.

At the end of the song, flames shot into the air and KISS's amps blew up. I was a rabid new fan. This band was going to destroy everything in my life that was dumb and boring. KISS was a gang I wanted to join. And I really needed a guitar.

I had to get my hands on their records—but I didn't have any money. I raced down to the local head shop. The hippie behind the counter was happy to trade me a couple KISS albums for my Elton John and Peter Frampton records.

Chapter 6

7 Train to Glory

I've been watching the rain
I've been learning to fall
Like a natural
—"Lowlife in a High Rise"

After seeing KISS on TV, I was desperate for a guitar. My father got me a cheap acoustic—but I wanted to dive right into playing loud electric guitar and jumping around.

A nice Mexican girl in my class loaned me her brother's electric guitar and little practice amp for a week. That guitar sounded so big and loud when I plugged it in. I couldn't keep it in tune, or play chords very well with my tiny fingers, but the sound of it blasting through that amp had such power. It was even more exciting than singing into the microphone my mother used to run through the stereo in our old living room.

I begged my mother for an electric guitar, but she couldn't afford to buy me one. So I dug around in Papa Artie's basement. I found a flat microphone and a rusty reel-to-reel tape machine with built-in speakers. I lugged this stuff home.

In my bedroom, I Scotch-taped the mic onto my acoustic guitar, near the bridge. The mic kept sliding off, so I switched to masking tape. I plugged the mic cable into the tape machine and strummed my guitar. The sound that came through those crappy little speakers wasn't great, but it was real loud and even kind of warm.

Better close my door, I thought.

I grabbed the brass knob while holding my makeshift

electric guitar, and got zapped by a powerful shock that nearly knocked me over. Undeterred, I played my dangerous little contraption every day after school. It even made cool squealing feedback sometimes that sounded like Jimi Hendrix.

I kept yelling for a real electric guitar, though. Finally, my mother's new boyfriend, Frank Shira, bought me a Les Paul copy for under a hundred bucks. I was a little embarrassed that it said *Memphis* on the headstock, instead of *Gibson*. But it had a beautiful black shine, like Ace Frehley's guitar on TV. I was really happy to have it.

Frank owned a local gas station. He looked a bit like an Israeli version of Uncle Frank in *Tommy*. Frank had a huge smile and was always laughing. My mother liked him a lot, and so did I. Frank had a wife, though, and two kids.

Frank's daughter, Jade, was only twelve, but she already had boobs and some teenage swagger. On July 4, my mother, Juliet, and I piled into Frank's car to go see the fireworks up on Suicide Hill. Jade and I were in the backseat, and she kept pinching my ass.

What the hell's going on here? I wondered.

I was eleven, and at the mercy of mind-warping puberty. I was flooded with testosterone and obsessed with any female body part I glimpsed on HBO at my dad's apartment, or in the R-rated movies my friends and I snuck into at the Quartet. We'd pay for a PG, and then scurry into *The Kentucky Fried Movie* so we could stare awestruck at some hot actress's big boobs pressed up against a glass shower wall.

Sex was everywhere in the 1970s. There was this playful impression that it didn't really do any harm. Even the pornos had a sense of humor. I saw an ad in the paper for *The Erotic Adventures of Pinocchio*: *It's not his nose that grows. See the surprise when he lies!* Sometimes I'd find a *Penthouse Forum* or an erotic novel in my mother's bottom dresser drawer, which I'd quickly spirit into the bathroom. But I was burning up to do the mystery dance for real.

My mother was a vivacious brunette who loved to go out and have fun. She and her favorite cousin, Joanie, joked about sex a lot. They'd be having a drink in the living room, getting ready to go out, and my mother would say something like, "I used to date this guy in high school. *I don't got a convertible*, he'd say, *I got a pervertible. The top don't go down, but the driver does!*" And Joanie and my mother would howl with laughter.

If my mother was regaling Joanie with a story about her new boyfriend, Joanie would yell, "He betta have a big one!" All my mom's friends and relatives cracked wise about sex in this rowdy, no-filter, Lenny Bruce, New York Jewish kinda way.

A hot blond teenage girl moved into the apartment next door. My friend Steven Avalon and I figured out that her bedroom shared a wall with my sister's half of our bedroom.

Juliet's side was sweet and innocent, with stuffed animals on her little bed, and a couple of shelves that held her children's books and toys. My side was rock and roll. KISS and Zeppelin posters were taped to the wall above my bed. It was strewn with my favorite albums, copies of *Circus* and *Creem*, and the comics I was reading.

The most important thing in my life, besides my electric guitar, was a thin bamboo shade that split our bedroom in half and provided some semblance of privacy. I called it the Divider.

Steven and I snuck a drill out of his dad's toolbox. While my sister was playing at a friend's house, I cranked up Ted Nugent's *Cat Scratch Fever* to hide the racket as we drilled a hole into the wall above my sister's bed so we could spy on the hot girl. To our frustration, we didn't get very far, as the wall was about two feet thick.

Undeterred, we dug a hammer out of the toolbox, and searched his father's car trunk for a more effective weapon of destruction. We found a crowbar, and whenever my mother and sister were out of the apartment, we banged on that hole like we were trying to bust out of prison. We covered our deviant handiwork with a Frank Zappa poster.

One day, we finally broke through. But instead of the neat little peephole we had planned to create, we had completely wrecked the wall and ripped through a painting in the poor girl's bedroom. As soon as her mother came home and discovered the mess, she began ringing the doorbell to my apartment and pounding on the door.

My mother wasn't home, thank God, so I huddled in the bathroom until our neighbor finally went away. I got busted, of course, and was grounded for a month.

Being grounded gave me time to think, and to plan. On the day I wasn't grounded anymore, I put my plan into action.

"Love Gun" by KISS blasted from my record player as I got dressed. The card Grandma Sara had sent me for my eleventh birthday lay on top of the small wooden dresser that had followed me everywhere I'd lived so far. Next to the card were a subway token, my keys, some change, and the black leather gloves with gold zippers up the back that I had begged my mother to buy for me so I could look tough like Gene Simmons.

I pulled on black Lee jeans and threaded my prized silver-studded belt through the loops, because even though I was a card-carrying member of the KISS Army, I had recently discovered punk rock. I sat on my narrow bed and laced up the new work boots I had gotten at the Army Navy store on Bell Boulevard in Bayside. I opened a drawer, rummaged through my tube socks and underwear, and dug out the buck knife I bought there, too, while my mother wasn't looking. I slid it into my back pocket.

I rolled up my white T-shirt sleeves like the Fonz and slipped on my black vinyl motorcycle jacket. I put on my gloves and pulled the zippers tight. I slipped the twenty-five dollars out of Grandma Sara's birthday card and put it in my right jacket pocket. I zipped that up tight, too. I slid the token, keys, and change off the dresser and into my jean pockets. I was ready for my mission.

It was a chilly March day, damp and gray. I walked across the street to the 166th Street bus stop and paced back and forth until the bus arrived. I've never been good at standing still. When the bus pulled up, I dropped two quarters into the fare box and ambled to the back.

The back bench is always hot from the engine, which feels good on a cold day, but it smells foul because drivers piss out the back door, drenching the stairs in urine. You need a strong stomach to sit there huffing diesel-piss fumes while the bus lurches to a stop every few blocks.

The bus takes thirty-five minutes to get to Flushing–Main Street. It's bustling with shoppers rushing in and out of department stores, movie theaters, record stores, and head shops. When I'm with my buddy Steven Avalon, we go to Jolly Joint, a head shop that sells Rush, which we sniff. Then we race by the newsstands grabbing porno magazines, high as kites and cackling like hyenas.

But not today. Today, I need to stay focused.

I exit the bus and hustle down concrete stairs into the Flushing–Main Street subway station. I drop my token in the turnstile slot and push through. Crackling, indecipherable announcements blare out of tinny speakers. A graffiti-bombed train pulls into the station and I hop on board.

Graffiti completely covers the inside of the train, too. Every metal wall, every window, every door is densely tagged with thick black marker and overlapping layers of spray paint. Artist on top of artist. Not an inch of real estate wasted as the taggers duke it out.

As the train rises above ground near Shea Stadium, it trundles past the junkyards lining Willets Point. That's when my friends and I like to haul open the doors between cars, climb on top of the train, and make like surfers before it dives back underground.

Now, though, I stay in my seat, avoiding eye contact with the owners of various groins and armpits that wind up in my face; shrinking my shoulders away from the greasy-haired fat guy squashed in next to me. Sixteen stops later, the train comes to a shrieking halt at 42nd Street.

I bound up the stairs thinking I'm the coolest kid in New York. There, spread before me, is pre-Disney Times Square in all her dirty, insolent glory, looking like every crime movie I've ever seen and everything I want. Theaters line either side of 42nd Street forever. Lurid red and black letters on white marquees offer *Satan's Mistress*, *Flesh Gordon*, *The Filthy 5*, *Swedish Minx*, *Challenge of the Ninja*. Sidewalk boards shout *Live Nude Girls! Live Sex Shows!* My head swivels as I take in the larger-than-life photos of strippers in G-strings posted outside the topless bars. My mother would murder me—if she only knew.

Times Square is the ultimate sex-and-violence theme park. Not a family amusement park like Six Flags, which I used to dash into straight from the family car like a hyped-up dog, eager for the thrill of the scariest roller coaster. Nope, the Deuce is where I'm going to get laid, because I've got twenty-five dollars in my pocket and I want it all.

As if they've read my mind, two twenty-something brothers emerge from underneath a porno marquee and walk straight toward me. They're clad in long overcoats made of heavy suede, festooned with fringe. One dude is wearing a wool ski cap.

"Yo, homie, you want some women? You need some women?"

Wow, this is awesome. How did they know? I nod eagerly, "Yeah!"

"Come with us," Ski Cap says. "We got you, bro. We got you."

I follow my new friends down 42nd Street to Eighth Avenue. We dodge scammers running three-card-monte hustles, drunks passed out cold, and hookers on the stroll in tight miniskirts and patent-vinyl thigh-high boots.

We hang a right near the Port Authority Bus Terminal. As the avenue opens wide, the vibe gets more hardcore. We pass twenty-five-cent peep shows and fenced-off vacant lots full of trash. An enormous rat saunters across our path. I'm a little scared, but blown away by my great luck. Clearly, God wants me to have sex.

We stop at a doorway next to a peep joint. My guides open the door and usher me inside. We climb two flights of chipped marble stairs to a dark landing. Ski Cap points to a black door. "This is where the ladies at," he declares. "We gonna leave, 'cause this shit is illegal. You gonna wait for that door to open and then you can go inside and bust that nut." He looks me up and down. "Got any weapons, bro? Can't bring in no weapons."

I nod understandingly, and solemnly hand him my buck knife. The other guy eyes my studded belt. "That looks kinda dangerous, homie."

I take off my belt and give it to him.

"Take off them gloves, too," he says, "and your jacket."

I hesitate.

"Bro, we got you," he murmurs. "No sweat, we'll hold your shit tight and bring it back when you done."

Horniness wins: I hand over my gloves and jacket.

"Where's the money?" Ski Cap says.

"This is all I got," I reply, digging awkwardly into my jacket, which is draped over his buddy's arm. I hold out my twenty-five bucks hopefully.

Ski Cap frowns. "The lady's time cost forty, bro. You ain't got no more?"

"This is everything," I say.

Ski Cap takes the money, to my great relief.

"All right, bro, you wait here. We'll be back. You chill and the lady's gonna let you in real soon. You're gonna have a real great time."

They slip down the stairs.

I am so freaking excited that I barely notice. I'm sweating, my heart is pounding. Finally, it's gonna happen. Sex! Yeah! What should I do? I keep thinking about what I've seen in dirty magazines.

Five minutes whiz by as my sex-crazed imagination runs wild. Then ten. Time slows to a crawl as I fixate on that door. Cautiously, I pull the handle. The door is locked. Fifteen minutes pass. Twenty. I knock on the door. Nothing. I bang harder, panic rising in my throat.

Nobody comes. I am standing alone in the dark at the top of a deserted stairwell on Eighth Avenue. It finally hits me: That door is never going to open. Those dudes have taken all my shit. I've been robbed.

How am I going to get home?

To this day, I'd like to thank those guys for stealing my stuff—and saving my innocence.

Chapter 7

Fast Kiss

*My parents felt the same
But they'd never admit it*
—"All the Way from Moscow"

Nearly every kid's parents were divorced in my neighborhood. Women were leaving their marriages in droves, freed by the pill and the ability to earn their own money. Like the song said, they could finally "*Do it. Do it. Do it. Do the Hustle!*"

I felt this big shift as marriages cracked up, bombs exploded in Vietnam on TV, and New York City degenerated into a dirty, savage, apocalyptic mess. There was a wildness but also a freedom when everything fell apart.

The city was broke. People who could afford to leave fled for the suburbs. Mountains of stinking garbage piled up in front of burnt-out buildings. The sidewalks were covered in dog shit. Rusty abandoned cars littered the streets. The power went out across nearly the entire city for two days in the summer of 1977. Rats, arsonists, looters, and muggers ran amok. So did a serial killer who was shooting young couples in parked cars. He called himself "Son of Sam."

It was a free-for-all. And it felt like nobody cared. I still remember the *Daily News* headline after the president refused to save New York from bankruptcy: "FORD TO CITY: DROP DEAD."

But behind the old brick buildings in Whitestone ran the

East River. My mother was always drawn to the water, and found peace there. She used to go down to a beat-up old dock sometimes and sing out loud when no one was around. She used to cry down there, too.

Still, no matter how broke we were, my mother kept our spirits up, laughing and joking around. She always believed in a better tomorrow. A little yellow sign with a flower painted on it hung above our kitchen sink: TODAY IS THE FIRST DAY OF THE REST OF YOUR LIFE.

My mother, Joanie, and Uncle Jon hit the town together on the weekends, partying at discos and singles bars. After Grandma Renee died of cancer at fifty-five, Papa Artie, who was lonely and looked very young for his age, joined them, too.

They had each other's backs. If one of them got lucky, great! If somebody got too drunk, they made sure he or she got home safely.

Well, sort of.

One night, Uncle Jon drank four vodka sodas in a row and was feeling pretty good. "You're drunk as a skunk!" Joanie shouted. "You betta go home!" They all walked Uncle Jon out to the parking lot, carefully put him in his car, and waved goodbye as he drove off.

That's how it was done in the seventies.

My mother seemed happy to be free of my dad, even though we never had enough money. But sometimes in the middle of the night I'd hear her crying . . . softly.

Concerned, I'd tiptoe out of my bedroom and peer around the corner into the darkness, only to discover that she wasn't crying at all. She was moaning with pleasure, writhing naked underneath her boyfriend on a sheet and some pillows they had dragged onto the living-room carpet.

I would freeze, my heart racing. I'd stand in the dark listening feverishly, feeling sick to my stomach—but turned on at the same time. A part of me wanted to run away, and a part of me wanted to stay.

What was this sex thing all about? I was still desperate to know.

On the bus, boys boasted about their conquests, and compared notes on which girls put out. At school, stoners wandered the halls asking, "Got anything for the head?"

I tried asking out girls at school, but they laughed at me. I was an awkward wannabe-rocker with long brown curls obscuring my pale face, and they were little disco queens poured into skintight Jordache jeans. They preferred the Italian boys wearing silky polyester shirts and gold chains who strutted down the halls like Tony Manero in *Saturday Night Fever*.

Only one girl who was into disco ever liked me: Maria Lagarelli. She was a beautiful young Bo Derek type with blue eyes and a mischievous smile. Maria kept giving me the eye in the hallway until I got up the nerve to approach her. She lived near school, so I began walking her home after class. I even got a fast kiss.

Maria was on my mind pretty heavy one night, so I went over to her neighborhood to see if she was around. A couple of tough-looking Italian teenagers were hanging out on the block.

"Whatcha doin' here?" one barked.

"I'm looking for Maria," I said.

"Oh yeah? We're her brothers," the other one said.

They looked me up and down, clearly not impressed with my long hair and the chains wrapped around my boots. They grabbed me and steered me back to the schoolyard, where they beat me pretty bloody.

That was the last time I tried to call for Maria, or walk her home. I left the dried blood on my jacket for months to remind me to get out the fuck out of Whitestone as soon as possible.

* * *

That summer, my mother sent me to Clearview Day Camp, which was held at a local public school. I didn't want to spend my time off anywhere near a classroom—until I met a cute girl at camp named Lucy Pollard. She liked KISS, which clinched the deal for me. We fooled around behind the pool lockers, and it was such a beautiful rush, something magical and warm that I had never felt before.

When Lucy dumped me out of the blue midsummer, I was crushed. I didn't know what to do. Her friend Mary Rispoli had a thing for me, so I went for it. A camp counselor caught us making out under the boardwalk on a trip to the beach. He stood me in front of everyone in my wet bathing suit and beat my ass with a Wiffle ball bat until I fell down with tears in my eyes.

But one afternoon when my mother and sister weren't home, Jade Shira came over. She kept sitting closer and closer to me on my bed until she was rubbing my thighs and getting me all worked up. We started having sex and I came really fast.

"Fuck, that was terrible!" Jade sneered. "You're terrible. That really sucked."

She left in a huff. After that, she stopped pinching my ass or trying to get me alone. I called her a few times, but she never answered. It really messed me up. After losing my virginity so awkwardly to Jade, I felt too traumatized to try to have sex with anybody else for a while.

Years later, I told a girlfriend this story and she said, "Somebody must have done something to her when she was way too young."

That rang true.

Chapter 8

Last Car on the Line

*From the alleys to the valley
See 'em riding just like Sally*
—"No Way Out"

When I was a kid, it was all about the phone. Not a cell phone in my pocket; we didn't have those back then. One landline at home. Or a dirty pay phone on the corner. You'd beam a message out into the universe and pray that something exciting would come bouncing back. I'd get home from school and yell, "Ma, did anybody call?"

I still loved KISS, but after seeing the Sex Pistols on TV, I had fallen hard for punk rock. The Sex Pistols were raw, fast, loud. So much angrier than KISS. Skinny, pissed-off live wires, just like I was. *Never Mind the Bollocks* made me want to bust up my entire bedroom—like when Matt and I were kids and we'd get a new toy and read the glee in each other's eyes: "Let's break it!"

I was in junior high at P.S. 194 on 17th Avenue, where I freaked out my teachers and alienated my classmates by spiking my hair with K-Y Jelly, and stomping around like Johnny Rotten in brothel creepers—black-suede shoes with extra-thick crepe soles. I lived in black bondage pants and my ever-present leather jacket.

"What are those fucking retard shoes?" my father scoffed when he came to visit. "You look like fucking Mother Goose."

"Your boy Elvis wore them!" I protested. "They're brothel creepers." I didn't know what a brothel was, to tell the truth. I didn't know what bondage was either, for that matter.

If my mother told me Jimmy Drescher had called, I'd call him right back. Jimmy was a rowdy kid from Astoria who was also into punk. He would take the R train to Queensboro Plaza, and I'd look for him in the last car of every train as it pulled up to the platform. When I saw Jimmy, I'd jump in. That's how we met up—in the last car on the line.

Jimmy and I rode into the city together to prowl dusty indie record stores in the West Village. The record store owners were loudmouthed, music-crazed maniacs with names like Bleecker Bob and Broadway Al. They blasted all kinds of fantastic music we'd never heard before.

Bleecker Bob might scream over the din, "If ya dig that, check out this!" and crank up *Raw Power* by the Stooges, or something by the New York Dolls. When the Ramones roared out of the speakers, that was like caveman music from outer space. "Blitzkrieg Bop," "Teenage Lobotomy." Those songs were tough, fast, and primitive. I was hooked. Once I heard the Ramones, all the hours I'd spent trying to play "Stairway to Heaven" on the guitar went out the window. I learned a few Ramones songs and realized maybe I could write songs, too. That was more exciting to me than anything.

Jimmy and I collided with other punk kids in record stores and hung out on tenement stoops drinking cheap beers from brown paper bags. We ran all over town, looking for fun, getting into trouble, and invariably losing each other in the night.

I'd finally take the R back to Queensboro Plaza alone, where I'd have to wait forever for the 7 train. Bored and exhausted, I'd wander around the outdoor platform, staring down at the dirty streets. I could see hookers getting into cars and turning tricks right outside in the alleys underneath the 59th Street Bridge. It made me think about what a person might have to do to get by in this world. It made me sad.

The next day, my buddies and I would call each other up and trade adventures.

"Dude, I ended up getting it on with a chick in the back of a car on Avenue D!"

"We passed out in the sandbox in Washington Square Park."

"I spent the night on that girl's floor. The chick with the spiky black hair."

"Whoa, she was hot! Did she give ya any action?"

"Nah..."

The Ramones were from Queens, and that meant something to me. I got Joey Ramone's phone number from a Whitestone girl who was a superfan.

I would call Joey around noon, when he was waking up, and pester him with questions about music, which he answered patiently. I'll always be grateful for how kind he was to a pesky twelve-year-old.

"Hey, Joey, it's Jesse!"

"Hey, Jesse, what's up?"

"Whaddya think about Johnny Thunders and the Heartbreakers?"

"They're junkies!" he sneered. I didn't know that "junkie" meant heroin addict. I thought maybe it was somebody who ate too many Twinkies, because I loved the song "Junk Food Junkie" by Larry Groce.

"What about Elvis Costello? You like him? What about Joe Jackson?"

"Ahh . . ." Joey groaned. "They're all English guys trying to be Bruce Springsteen."

I didn't get what Joey meant by that either. In their sharp suits and skinny ties, Elvis Costello and Joe Jackson looked really different from that scruffy guy in blue jeans. But today, I get it. Coming up in the UK pub scene, Costello and Jackson probably cut their teeth on the same records that Springsteen loved.

When I heard that the Ramones movie *Rock 'n' Roll High School* was opening at the 8th Street Playhouse in Manhattan, I had to go. I got out of the subway at Broadway and 8th and promptly set off in the wrong direction. As I walked east, the street sign abruptly changed from *8th Street* to *St. Marks Place*. That freaked me out. Where the hell was I?

The moment I crossed Third Avenue, I entered a punk-rock *Sesame Street* crawling with spiky-haired creatures in leather jackets, rockers in sharp suits, Rastas with swinging dreads, hippies, and big scary bikers. Some sleazy guy got right in my face, chanting, "Coke, dope, blues, reds. Coke, dope, blues, reds."

I stopped to stare at punked-out mannequins in the windows at Trash and Vaudeville, and striped mohair sweaters and studded leather belts on display at Manic Panic. I couldn't believe a place like this really existed.

There was excitement and danger in the air, so naturally I kept walking. As I reached Second Avenue, I saw people sitting on the sidewalks selling used clothes and records laid out on old bedsheets. I sensed hardness and desperation, but also a freedom I had never felt before. I walked as far as First Avenue before I got scared and turned around. I knew this was where I belonged. I'd be back one day, as soon as I got up the guts.

But right now, I had to find that theater. I turned around

and sprinted west, praying I was going the right way this time. I finally reached the 8th Street Playhouse and got in line behind three teenagers dressed in black like me.

"You like the Ramones?" one asked, pointing at my *Rocket to Russia* T-shirt.

"Yeah!" I said.

"You ever heard of the Clash?"

"Yeah."

"They're even better!"

"No way," I declared. "Nobody's better than the Ramones."

Suddenly, to my surprise, I spotted Johnny Ramone across the street. He was walking with a pretty blonde—scoping out the movie marquee on opening day. I couldn't believe it.

I raced across the street, dodging cars, and ran up to Johnny to say hello. He was super friendly, and he had a strong Queens accent, just like everybody in my neighborhood.

I was even more thrilled to see *Rock 'n' Roll High School* after meeting a Ramone. Clearly, the city had some kind of magic and anything was possible. I started going to St. Marks Place whenever I could, coming home with imported records, fanzines, studded leather wristbands, and punk T-shirts.

Older kids would see me getting off the bus in Whitestone with my hot-pink Trash and Vaudeville bag and yell, "Hey, Malin, where ya comin' from . . . THE VILLAGE?" As if I'd been cruising around Christopher Street dancing to "Macho Man" with the Village People. Which would have been fun, too.

On New Year's Eve 1979, I told my mother I was going to a neighborhood party. Instead, I took the subway to Manhattan to see the Ramones at the Palladium.

Most of my life had taken place in the 1970s, so heading into 1980 felt like a thrilling trip into the magical future that

I deserved to kick off with a special occasion. At least that's what I told myself to shove aside my guilt about lying to my mother, who was home nursing a broken arm after falling at the roller rink.

The Palladium was a decaying old theater palace on 14th Street and Irving Place that held around three thousand people. The backstage door was on 13th Street. If you got there early, and stood around long enough, you might see the band arrive and maybe get an autograph, or even sneak into the show.

I hung around until I spotted Monte Melnick, the Ramones's tour manager. With his handlebar mustache, leather jacket, and aviator glasses, Monte looked like a seventies porno actor. He dangled a backstage pass and I gave him all the money I had, twenty bucks. Clearly, I had learned nothing from my trip to Times Square.

I felt incredibly cool walking up the loading dock into the Palladium with a backstage pass stuck on my pants. An usher kicked me out of my seat for not having a ticket, so I watched most of *Rock 'n' Roll High School*—which was being shown before the band's gig—from the wings with three thousand screaming, wisecracking New Yorkers. I had already seen it, of course, but I didn't care. I could have watched it a million times.

After the movie, a military drum roll began to play, really loud. Anticipation built as the crowd chanted, "*Hey! Ho! Let's go! Hey! Ho! Let's go!*" Finally, the Ramones walked onstage, looking like the coolest band on the planet.

At six foot six, Joey's arms were so long that the sleeves on his black-leather motorcycle jacket only came to the middle of his forearms. He draped his pale fingers over the mic and screamed, "Yeahhh you got it, we are the Ramones!"

Bass player Dee Dee shouted, "One, two, three, four!"

and the Ramones were off. They didn't let up for a second, ripping from one great song into the next, playing even faster than on their records. An amp blew up, and a roadie in a Pinhead mask marched around onstage with a huge sign that read GABBA GABBA HEY! on one side and HAPPY NEW YEAR! on the other.

"It's one minute to midnight!" Joey yelled. The Ramones roared into "Do You Wanna Dance?" as balloons dropped all over the audience from the ceiling. I was wowed.

I spilled out with the rest of the crowd into the chaotic electric energy of New York City celebrating the arrival of the 1980s. All the cabs and cars were honking. Drunk people in party clothes hung out of car windows screaming and waving. The sidewalks were packed with people smashing bottles, tooting noisemakers, grabbing each other, hugging and kissing. New Yorkers were going bananas. You could feel change in the air. It was the end of the sexy, earthy seventies. The age of video games, drum machines, synths, and spandex was dawning. The future was here.

I found myself near Disco Donut—the sketchy coffee shop where Travis takes Iris in *Taxi Driver. Oh shit*, I realized, *I gave Monte all my money. How am I going to get home?*

I started to panic. It was very late, and I was going to be in deep trouble for lying to my mother. I walked to the Union Square subway station on 14th Street. I didn't spot any cops on the platform so I slipped under the turnstile real quick.

I climbed out of the subway at Flushing–Main Street around three a.m. I thought about pulling a runner out of the back of a cab to get home. I had done that a few times, even though I knew how mean it was to cheat the driver of their fare. I didn't think I could cope with the guilt of shafting a cabbie on top of lying to my mother. I walked the five miles to my apartment building down sidewalks littered with broken bottles, confetti, and puke.

I carefully turned my key in the front-door lock, hoping to sneak in while my mother was sleeping so she'd never be the wiser. I made it into my bed without waking her and passed out. The next morning, she screamed at me that my friend Anthony Carizzi had ratted me out. I was grounded for a month. Again.

I was so mad that I called Carizzi and threatened to beat him up. His father, a tough old-school Italian with big warts on his face, called me back and growled, "If you ever touch my son, I'm gonna bite your dick off, chew it up, and spit it in your face."

Sometimes not-so-good energy came through the phone.

I valued my penis, so Carizzi and I stopped being friends. We reconnected a few years later, when we ran into each other at some hardcore shows on the Lower East Side. Anthony had become an Italian-Jewish punk-rock Rastafarian, and our friendship was renewed.

A few months after seeing the Ramones at the Palladium, I went back to try to meet the Clash. I arrived early, and waited eagerly outside that stage door. Some bratty little kid with spiky hair, wearing plaid bondage pants, pushed in front of me. I was about to shove him back when the Clash's bass player, Paul Simonon, came out. He signed my ticket and said hello.

I was over the moon. But then Simonon ushered the bratty little kid into the Palladium, and left me standing on the sidewalk.

Who the hell is that guy? I fumed.

I asked around and found out he was Harley Flanagan,

the drummer in a new cool band called the Stimulators. And he was the same age as I was.

Fuck, I thought, *if he can do it, I can do it.*

Chapter 9

Making a Scene

*I found another path
Through the broken glass*
—"Shining Down"

I decided to start a punk band called Heart Attack. I figured a heart attack was the highest peak of adrenaline you could reach. Like, you get so amped up that . . . you have a heart attack!

Angus Young from AC/DC was one of my favorite guitar players. I loved how thick and tough his Gibson SG sounded. I needed that sound for Heart Attack. I had to figure out how to make some money, and I wanted to help my mom out, too.

I got a job for myself and Matt distributing fliers for a local dog-grooming shop called the Dog Shack. We were supposed to cover thirty-four buildings in our neighborhood.

"How's he gonna know if we don't give them all out?" I told Matt after we hit a few buildings. "Let's just throw them down the incinerator."

So we did. And a few days later we were fired. I always wondered how that Dog Shack guy found out.

Next, I delivered newspapers. A man in a suit came to pick up me and a bunch of other boys at five in the morning. He drove us to the Bronx to deliver the *Daily News* throughout Co-op City—an overwhelming complex of real tall buildings. Wandering around those long, dank hallways, I feared I was going to get sucked into some creep's apartment, never to be seen again. A lot of those newspapers wound up in the incinerator, too.

My most successful childhood job was stealing for Jimmy, a teenager with greasy brown hair who came around in a beat-up Mustang, blasting Bad Company on his eight-track tape player. Jimmy drove me, my friend Brandon Lewis, and a couple other kids from the neighborhood to places like Genovese Drug Store, and sent us in to steal stuff.

"Get the whole carton!" he'd yell over the music, when he dropped us off.

We ransacked those stores, stuffing our pants, shirts, and hoodies full of gum, batteries, cigarettes, condoms—anything we could get our hands on. Jimmy paid us a few bucks and gave us a couple packs of gum sometimes, if we were lucky. I felt like a cool criminal in a movie, tearing around Queens in a loud, fast car pulling off our little heists to "Can't Get Enough."

Eventually, I saved up enough money to buy a cheap SG copy that sounded pretty good. I was ready for the stage. I just needed some partners in crime.

I looked for any kid at school who played an instrument. Henry Camus played piano. Better yet, his father had a drum kit, so I made Henry the drummer in my band.

Now we needed somewhere to rehearse. A few kids from school lived in real houses in Whitestone, instead of apartments. John Valdastri's family had a nice basement, and a pool.

"You wanna be my band's manager?" I asked him.

"Yeah!" John said.

"Great! Hmm . . . we need somewhere to rehearse."

"How 'bout my basement?"

"Perfect," I said.

Our noisy racket pissed off his parents real fast, though, and we were quickly kicked out.

Meanwhile, I had befriended a quiet, nerdy kid named John Jones. John stuck out like a sore thumb at school. He looked like a transplant from the 1950s in his crew cut, Sears blue jeans, and white T-shirt.

Other kids made fun of John for his plain clothes and military haircut. He was an outsider, like me. So even though John knew nothing about punk—or even rock and roll—I looked out for him. He was shy, but nice once you got to know him.

John's parents never let him go anywhere. He always had to head straight home after school. He never went out, even on weekends. John's stepfather was a big, tough corrections officer at Rikers. It was clear that John was afraid of him. But John's house had a garage, so that became Heart Attack's next rehearsal space. We moved in our rickety drum kit, my tiny solid-state amp, and the RadioShack microphone I had taped to a makeshift stand. We ran the mic through a battered bass amp.

John's stepfather wasn't home enough to notice, luckily, and his mother never came near us. There was a deadness emanating from the house, a weird energy I could feel even out in the garage.

We spent hours there that winter—freezing our asses off, drinking beer, blasting a boom box, and trying to figure out how to play songs. For a minute, it felt like John was part of our gang.

But every evening, John's mother would scream from the house, "Come on, Johnny! You gotta come in now. The Duke boys are on! The Duke boys!" John would have to leave us, and run inside to watch this goofy TV show, *The Dukes of Hazzard*, with his mother. He got this distant, disconnected look in his eyes when his mother called him.

I invited John to come see the new Cheech & Chong movie at the shopping center up the block. His mother said no because he would be out past his bedtime. I couldn't believe John couldn't go to an eight o'clock movie on a Saturday night.

His stepfather finally kicked us out of the garage, and John and I drifted apart, like kids do. A few years later, I ran into someone from P.S. 194.

"Hey, didja hear?" he said. "That weird guy John Jones shot his mother in the head!"

The real story was a little different. The *Daily News* reported that Mrs. Jones had come home and found John and his friend Tommy in John's bedroom, playing with Mr. Jones's pistol. John turned to Tommy and said, "Scare my mother." Tommy fired two shots. One hit Mrs. Jones in the face, killing her. Her body was found outside the house on the landing, wrapped in a bedspread, with a blood-soaked towel over her face.

John took the family dog and his little brother, and drove upstate. He was caught near Monroe when the car got stuck in mud. John and Tommy got twenty-five years each for second-degree murder.

I spotted a flier at Jolly Joint one day posted by a guy looking to play guitar in a punk band, and called him up. That's how I met Jack Flanagan.

Jack was a tall, heavyset kid with red hair and freckles, a few years older than me. He wore dog tags, and lived in camouflage pants and red Converse sneakers.

"Look," Jack said, pulling up his pant leg, "Legs McNeil signed my sneaker."

I had no idea who Legs McNeil was.

"You like the Ramones and the Dead Boys, right?" Jack added. "Check out this record from the Heartbreakers."

He cued up *Live at Max's Kansas City* on my record player. It was an incredibly raw album; I'd never heard anything like it. Singers Johnny Thunders and Walter Lure cursed each other out and cracked jokes about other bands in between knocking out super-catchy songs with pounding drums and nasty guitars, like "Get Off the Phone" and "Chinese Rocks."

"This is what we should sound like," Jack declared.

We started rehearsing in Jack's basement in Douglaston. I had some songs, he had some songs, and we got my fellow former shoplifter Brandon to play bass. Richie Ferrara was now on the drums. We were thirteen and Jack, at sixteen, was the old guy.

I heard that if you called up the punk club CBGB, you could book an audition on a Monday night and maybe even get a gig. I called from my junior high's only pay phone until I finally got through to a lady named Carol. She grudgingly gave Heart Attack a slot.

Our parents drove us to the Bowery in separate cars packed with our drum kit, guitars, and cheap Japanese solid-state amplifiers. By the time Heart Attack's little caravan reached CBGB, the sun had set. It was early spring, but still very cold.

CBGB was surrounded by broken-down flophouses. The sidewalks were strewn with red-faced drunks and junkies curling over in slow motion. Lost souls huddled in doorways, trying to escape the freezing wind. Half-dressed men staggered about. Some lurched straight toward us as we began to lug our gear across the sidewalk, forcing us to veer out of their semiconscious path. It was like *Night of the Living Dead* meets *Invasion of the Body Snatchers*.

Once we'd unloaded the cars, our folks took off. None of them wanted to stick around this scary scene to watch us make our debut.

The full name of the club was printed in red on a ratty white awning over its graffiti-covered entrance:

CBGB

OMFUG

I figured *OMFUG* meant something dirty. It never occurred to me to wonder what all those letters meant. I was shocked to find out later that they stood for *Country, Bluegrass and Blues, and Other Music for Uplifting Gourmandizers*. On the Bowery? What the hell were they thinking?

We dragged our gear past the zombies and into the club. It was dark inside, and smelled like piss, ammonia, stale beer, and dog shit. We lumbered along the narrow passage between the bar on our right and beat-up banquettes to our left with chunks of foam poking through the splits in their vinyl coverings. We finally reached the stage, which rose about four feet above the club's uneven wooden floor.

The staff was small and unfriendly. Nobody was out to make you feel special; in fact, they were cranky, and completely uninterested in you and your stupid band. To my disappointment, nobody was wearing any punk or rock-and-roll regalia.

Is this really the place in the magazines? I wondered. *The place where it all happened? Where Blondie, Talking Heads, and even AC/DC got their start? Well, the Ramones started out by dragging their stuff into this gloomy dive on a Monday night, too. This is how it's done, and I'm gonna do it.*

The skinny sound guy climbed onstage and began setting mics in front of our amps without saying a word. Perched on a ladder across from the stage was an angry bear of a man with a black mustache and thick chest hair sprouting from his tight white T-shirt. He "ran" the stage lights by pushing them around with a broken mic-stand pole.

"Yeeeaaah, we're gonna cook you with these cans!" he screeched as we were setting up. "We're gonna fry you with these lights! You boys are gonna buuuurn!"

Despite the weird vibe, I felt something profound when I stepped onto that legendary wooden stage. I could see that it had once been ragged and splintery, but over time all the feet that had danced across it had polished it to a smooth gleam—like petrified wood.

When Richie hit the kick drum, it sounded like a bomb exploding. That kick rumbled beneath my feet and rose through my body like nothing I had ever felt before. We were so loud. My heart was pounding. This was power.

We crashed chaotically into our short set, playing our songs at warp speed: "Young and Dangerous," "I Don't Want You Anymore," "Chains and Knives" and "KGB." I bounced all over the stage, determined to keep Heart Attack roaring nonstop from song to song, just like the Ramones. The lights were hot, and the volume was pounding. I was scared, hyped up, but also strangely comfortable. This was the adrenaline fix I'd been searching for my whole life—galaxies beyond sniffing Rush, kissing a girl, or sneaking into an R-rated picture.

We also did a crazed, punked-up version of "In the Still of the Night" by the Five Satins. I don't know what I was thinking, except that my father had drilled into my head that it was the number one song of all time on the *Top 500 Oldies Countdown*.

I peered into the dark, trying to see past the blinding stage lights. I could make out a few drunk people slouched at chairs and tables in front of the stage—but beyond that, all

I saw was pitch black, straight out to the Bowery. Even so, I just knew this was going to work.

Our performance was a fun but frantic mess. It flew by in a blur. Many gigs feel like that, especially early on, when adrenaline takes over because you haven't yet mastered riding the surges. The rehearsals, the travel, lugging in the gear, and setting up onstage are like the slow, clicking build of a roller coaster climbing that first steep hill. Then you zoom down in a blink and it's over.

Brandon, Richie, Jack, and I hopped offstage feeling amped to the nines, like we had accomplished something huge. I'd grown from smashing toys to channeling my rage into this—and it felt great.

It's still the same, even now. As much as the world changes, some things remain the same. There's still nothing like lacing your boots up real tight and standing in the dressing room with your heart pounding, until somebody says, "You're on, let's go!" and you know you can't run away. You've got to walk onstage and make it happen. You've got to play every show like you have a gun at your back. It's a thrilling, addictive mix of power and fear.

I got my first taste of blood that Monday night and I still can't get away from it.

I eagerly called the club from my house the next afternoon.

"Sorry, kid," Carol said flatly, "ya failed the audition."

"Wait, hold on," I responded. "Why?"

"Ah, you guys have missed the boat. Punk's over. It's dead. Try something new. Like rockabilly. Or New Romantic. Maybe synth-pop. I dunno. Besides, ya gotta bring at least twenty people."

I was seriously bummed.

But then, through the miracle of the telephone, Heart Attack was redeemed. A guy who booked Max's Kansas City had been at CBGB that night and saw us. He got my number and called my house.

"Jesse! You got a call from the city!" my mother screamed.

I ran into the kitchen and grabbed the phone from her.

"Hey, kid, you wanna play at Max's?"

Hell yeah, I wanted to play Max's! I booked our second gig for July 15, 1980.

Chapter 10

Chinese Wops

You walked around town with your collar up
And you never got off on that racist stuff
—"State of the Art"

I had been fascinated with Max's Kansas City ever since my mother took Juliet and me to see the circus at Madison Square Garden when we were little. On the drive home, we crawled slowly down Park Avenue South as packs of hookers in corsets and platform boots ran all over the street blocking traffic, catcalling cars, and screaming with laughter.

If that wasn't exciting enough, when we hit 18th Street, a crowd of the most outrageously cool people I'd ever seen were hanging out on the sidewalk in front of some nightclub. Printed in white ink on its wide black awning was: *Max's Kansas City*.

The scene outside Max's looked so decadent that I couldn't even imagine what might be going on inside. Mesmerized, I stared out the window thinking, *That's where I wanna be*.

After that, when I was bored in school—which was most of the time—I would draw a fake flier in my notebook for my imaginary rock band's show at Max's. I put a real date on the flier and everything. Then I'd stare at it real hard and determined. It's weird how often saying something out loud—or writing it down—can actually make it happen.

At home, I always had one leg off my chair at the kitchen table, ready to bolt out the door at any minute.

"Where do you think you're going, young man?" my mother would laugh.

I was pretty sure she wouldn't let me run all the way to Max's.

When I was eleven, I heard about a Whitestone kid who was actually living in the city. Howie Pyro was a local legend. Rumor had it he got his name from setting fires in the garages behind the Garden Apartments off Utopia Parkway. He worked in East Village clothing shops like Manic Panic and Trash and Vaudeville—crashing in their back rooms. Some girls in my neighborhood who hung out downtown always came back raving about how cool this Howie Pyro guy was.

There weren't many legends from Whitestone. Charlie Chaplin and Rudolph Valentino lived there in the 1920s. Dee Dee Ramone moved in when I was twelve. He copped drugs near my junior high after dark.

"Your boy came by last night to buy some shit!" a kid shouted at me in the schoolyard.

When I was twelve, I saw an ad in the *Village Voice* for "Hardcore Halloween" at Max's Kansas City. It was the first time I'd seen the word "hardcore" used anywhere outside of pornography. Dead Boys guitarist Cheetah Chrome was headlining. Some band called the Blessed was on the bill, too.

Brandon and I were huge Dead Boys fans. When Brandon's hip young mom offered to pick us up at one a.m. and drive us home, my mother agreed to let me go.

Brandon and I took the subway to Max's, and used our shoplifting money to pay the five-dollar cover charge. I tried to look tough and grown-up, but the doorman barely glanced at me as he took my cash. Nobody in New York checked IDs back then.

Brandon and I crammed as close to the stage as we could. The black curtain opened and there, standing right in front of me playing bass for the Blessed, was the coolest kid I'd ever seen. He had spiky jet-black hair and huge green eyes. His Danelectro Longhorn bass was slung low over his striped mohair sweater, black leather pants, and Converse high-top sneakers. It was that Whitestone legend, Howie Pyro.

The Blessed were the first teenage punk band on the New York scene. They played a fast, loose set. Howie was a star—bleeding swagger and attitude all over that stage. I never dreamed that one day he and I would be best friends, and have a band together.

Cheetah Chrome took forever to come on—probably busy doing drugs backstage. We only got to see three songs before Brandon's mom was outside, waiting to drive us home.

It was around this same time that the Blessed managed to secure an opening slot for the Damned's New York show. A dream gig. There was just one problem. Walter Lure from the Heartbreakers was playing guitar with the Blessed now, killing time while Johnny Thunders was strung out. The Heartbreakers had been on the UK Anarchy Tour with the Sex Pistols, the Damned, and the Clash.

"I'm not doing it!" Walter huffed. "The Damned used to open for us. Their roadies will laugh at me!"

The guys in the Blessed were crushed, but even back then, Howie tried to hook people up. He phoned some friends from New Jersey who had a new band called the Misfits, and offered them the Blessed's opening slot. Who would've thought that forty years later the Misfits would headline Madison Square Garden—and the Damned would be opening?

Anyway, that's why I was thrilled when Heart Attack was offered a gig at Max's. But I knew our parents didn't want to haul our equipment around ever again. How were we gonna get there?

I saw a flier at Waldbaum's supermarket for *Man with Van*.

Van Man turned out to be a wiry Irish guy in his late forties who lived right across the street from me. He wanted twenty-five bucks to drive us to the gig.

He pulled up in front of Jack's basement in a rusty white van, with a cigarette dangling from his mouth. We packed in our gear while he sat in the driver's seat drinking from a plaid thermos that stank of booze.

Van Man drove us over the 59th Street Bridge and headed downtown, while we bounced around in the back with our gear. As we careened down Park Avenue South toward Max's, he leaned out his window, screaming, "Get outta my way, bitches!" at the hookers.

Van Man parked in front of Max's, set up a lawn chair on the sidewalk, and pulled out a cooler. He sat there smoking and sucking down cans of beer as we dragged our equipment up the steep stairs to the second floor, where the bands played.

While I was setting up onstage, a sweaty, skinny guy in tight black jeans with really bad skin slouched over and tapped me on the shoulder. "Ya know what today is?" he whined, getting way too close.

"No idea," I muttered, annoyed.

"It's Johnny Thunders's birthday. You kids know any of his songs? 'Cause he's gonna show up tonight and wanna play. You betta be ready!"

"We know 'Chinese Rocks,'" I said.

"Yeah, that's cool. Maybe he'll do that one witcha. When he gets here, I'll give you guys the signal." He slouched off.

Closer to show time, my mother and aunt arrived to cheer us on. So did Jack Flanagan's mom and a crowd of Max's regulars. I was really pumped up, but I knew now that

I needed to control my energy and not go completely nuts when I hit the stage.

Halfway through our set—which was going great—that sweaty guy jumped onstage and spit in my face, "It's time! It's time! Let's go!" He grabbed my mic and we lurched into "Chinese Rocks."

I'm fully expecting Johnny Thunders to appear at any moment. We keep playing, with this pimple-faced idiot drooling onto my microphone, for nearly ten minutes. No Johnny Thunders.

I finally signal the band to stop. We slink offstage embarrassed, realizing we just got scammed by some freak. Immediately, my mother's in my face shouting, "Who is that guy? Do you know him? Is he on the heroin?"

"Ma, I don't know, I never met him before!"

"Is he a junkie? Is that part of your act?"

"Ma! I got no idea. I gotta pack up my stuff."

I drag my gear down the stairs and outside. Van Man is still in his lawn chair. He's stinking drunk and angry as hell.

"It's goddamn late, motherfucker," he slurs at me. "You said this was a matinee."

"Uh, sorry, we just finished," I say. "We're loading out right now."

"Fuck you!" he yells, sloshing a beer in my direction. "I'm leaving."

"No, wait, please," I say. "We'll be right out. Five minutes!" I race back inside to tell my bandmates to stop goofing around and load out ASAP.

But as I'm running through Max's first floor, I get distracted by all the video games lining the walls. Oooh... *Space Invaders*! As I head over to my favorite game, two muscular Asian guys in their twenties stalk over to me wearing black-satin baseball jackets—the kind popular with Staten Island

and Jersey rockers. Their silky black hair is cut into identical long shags.

These guys are even more pissed at me than Van Man—and I have no idea why. They pin me against the *Space Invaders* machine, leaning in so close that I can see the matching gold Italian horns dangling from matching chains around their necks. That puzzles me, but before I can even think about it, one guy slams his hand down hard on the console—*POW!*—right next to my head. I try not to flinch.

"What the fuck was that song you were singing, motherfucker?" he yells.

"I . . . what? Wha . . . what song?" I say.

The other guy slams his hand on the screen. "Chinese Wops!" he screams in my face. "Chinese WOPS?!"

Quickly, it dawns on me. These dudes must be Chinese *and* Italian. "No!" I yell. "It's called 'Chinese Rocks'! ROCKS! It's about drugs!"

While my new acquaintances ponder this information—no doubt trying to decide whether to beat me up anyway—I duck under their arms and dash upstairs.

As I rush in, Johnny Thunders swans into the room in a pink dinner jacket, his blue-black hair teased into a messy rooster-shag, a long thin scarf wrapped around his neck. Girls are kissing him and putting joints in his mouth. Guys slip pills into his pockets and hand him drinks.

Jack Flanagan pulls out his plastic Instamatic camera and hands it to some drunk screaming girl. She snaps a couple photos of me and Jack posing at the bar next to Johnny, who barely notices us. Then Johnny staggers onstage and launches into "Daddy Rolling Stone" with the band that went on right after Heart Attack.

I grab Brandon and Richie and we hurry downstairs with our gear and out into the street just as Van Man is pulling away. We bang on the vehicle until he unlocks the side door and lets us in. We pile in and rattle home to Queens perched on our amps, with a bombed Van Man at the wheel, shouting, "I thought this was a matinee! I thought this was a fucking matinee!"

Chapter 11

Mexico City

He was always about the music
Never smoked or drank
There was a singer down in DC that he used to thank
—"Bent Up"

P laying Max's proved to me that punk wasn't really dead. I didn't have to take Carol from CBGB's advice and turn Heart Attack into a synth-pop band. We weren't going to dress up like pirates or do the "Spandau Ballet." But Carol was right about one thing: we needed to do something new—something that would be ours.

I'd go to Jack's basement to rehearse, and he'd be blasting old Black Sabbath, and Ramones records sped up to 45 rpm. It sounded insane, but we loved it.

I rifled through the racks at record stores, trying to feed this raw sound I was craving. I wanted music that took no prisoners. Every day after school, I ran all over the apartment playing my songs as fast as I possibly could on my Japanese knockoff SG. Carol's words rang in my head: *Do something different.*

Jack started raving about a DC band called the Bad Brains who were coming to CBGB. I planned to be unimpressed. I figured they had nicked their name from the Ramones song "Bad Brain." That didn't seem too original to me.

The Bad Brains were all-Black, and the most blisteringly fast, ferociously tight band I had ever seen—with staggering jazz-fusion chops and the ability to stop on a dime. Handsome singer H.R. thrilled the twenty people there with backflips and raging kinetic energy, gliding across the stage in a tight gray suit, shimmying and shaking like James Brown on meth. The Bad Brains threw in a couple reggae tunes that got everybody skanking around the floor. H.R. could unleash a gut-wrenching scream like nobody else, but then he'd croon so beautifully on those reggae songs in a soft Jamaican accent. I was blown away.

A few weeks later, I saw AC/DC at the Palladium. After the show, I waited by the back door. Angus Young came out, but he didn't talk to anyone. He just danced around on top of a limo, then jumped in as it drove away.

Walking to the subway, I smelled weed coming from a parked van with its side door flung open. The Bad Brains were hanging out, giving away their first single. That's how I got "Pay to Cum" in a plain white sleeve.

"Pay to Cum" was ninety seconds of supersonic adrenaline. I listened to it over and over, trying to decipher the lyrics H.R. was spitting out faster than anyone I'd ever heard. I was convinced the Bad Brains couldn't play "Pay to Cum" that fast live—but they played it even faster.

Jack became completely obsessed with the Bad Brains. So obsessed that he started speaking like a Rastafarian and smoking weed. He quit Heart Attack and formed the Mob—"the fastest band in hardcore!"—with his Jackson Heights buddies.

Hardcore was this new punk sound that was louder, angrier, and faster than anything before. You had one minute to express everything you felt about the world—and I had a lot to say. Hardcore was that "something new" we needed. And it was ours.

I was mad at Jack for leaving, but when you're young and somebody splits, it pushes you to work twice as hard to show them up. I told myself Jack was too old, anyway. With just me on guitar, Heart Attack would be tighter and tougher.

The Mob put up fliers around Queens: *Be Rasta at Shamus Pub!* I went to check out the competition at the small Irish bar on Northern Boulevard.

Before every gig, the Bad Brains smoked weed together in their van outside the club—just vibing with each other. Before the Mob's show at Shamus Pub, I spotted Jack and his bandmates crammed into his mother's green Oldsmobile Toronado. It was so full of smoke that I could barely see them.

The Mob jumped onstage shouting, "Jah mon! Yes, boss! Croo-shee-all!" Just like the Bad Brains, they threw a few reggae songs into their set as well.

"You guys are Irish and Spanish kids from Queens!" I shouted at Jack afterward. "What the fuck?"

"Ah fuck you, Malin!" Jack yelled, dropping his fake Jamaican accent. "You're soft! The Mob blows Heart Attack away!"

When the Bad Brains played their reggae song "Leaving Babylon," H.R would shout, "Mash it! Mash down Babylon!"

Jack and the Mob's singer, Ralph Gebbia, misheard "mash" as "mosh." Ralphie would yell, "MOSH IT UP, MON" onstage while he and Jack shook their fists like little bears. They scrawled *Mosh it up Mob style!* on their fliers and everywhere. Their innocent mistake spread throughout the New York scene, and eventually all over the world.

Today, thanks to H.R. and two kids from Queens, dancers banging into each other at a show is called moshing, and the area in front of the stage will be forever known as the mosh pit.

When Black Flag played the Peppermint Lounge, I met a

bunch of DC punks, including Minor Threat singer Ian MacKaye. These guys had shaved heads and wrapped chains and bandannas around their boots. They wore plain T-shirts, flannels, and jeans, and unleashed the creepy-crawl dance on us New Yorkers. It was way more aggressive than our good-natured slam dancing. The DC punks squatted down low, swinging their arms like crabs, knocking people over. They steamrolled over everybody in the place. We were beaten down—but impressed. It was great meeting kids from another city who were into this music.

Minor Threat's antidrug song "Straight Edge" was even faster than "Pay to Cum." We all loved it. Hardcore was more than music to us. It was our community.

H.R. preached the power of a positive mental attitude (PMA) in the Bad Brains song "Attitude." He lived it with his ever-present smile and open heart. This was a big game changer for me and my friends—a huge step away from the dark drugs and nihilism of seventies punk. I've tried hard to keep the PMA ever since, even if I occasionally succumb to the NMA—Negative Malin Attitude.

DIY—do it yourself—became a credo for me, too. We didn't need to buy outfits from London anymore to be "punk." Don't advertise some famous band on your shirt. Take a Sharpie to your T-shirt, paint your jacket, and declare what you believe. Unplug the TV. Turn off mainstream radio. Fuck trying to "get signed." Start your own label. Make your own records, tapes, and fanzines.

And take care of each other—in the pit and on the street.

As hardcore spread, you could book a gig in somebody's basement, and find people who would let you crash on their floors. I couldn't wait to get Heart Attack on the road.

But not long after Jack left, so did Richie, our drummer. I could get by without a second guitarist, but not without a drummer. I put a classified ad in the *Village Voice* for a hardcore drummer, aged twelve to seventeen. Boy, did that bring out the creeps. My mother was fielding calls from middle-aged perverts panting to meet her thirteen-year-old son for an "audition."

One day, a guy with a heavy Spanish accent called. Javier Madariaga told me he was twenty, and had played in a Mexican punk band called Lujuria. He didn't seem too creepy, so I met him on 23rd Street and Third Avenue. Javier's black hair was cropped short. He wore leather pants, a black blazer, and a spiked leather bracelet. He looked closer to twenty-five than twenty.

"You look like a hippie-ippie-ippie," Javier sneered upon seeing me. "You look like a Ramone. They suck. Cut the hair. I'm into Sex Pistols. Real punk." He told me he was from Mexico City, and had lived in London. "Jesse," he asked very seriously, "do you trust yourself as a musician?"

I thought that was an interesting question. "Yeah!" I said.

"Good, 'cause I only wanna play with people that trust theyselves."

That was good enough for me. Javier was in. His fast tribal drumming gave my songs the fierce kick in the ass they'd been needing.

At this stage, I was working part-time at a Whitestone gas station to pay for rehearsals. Javier got a job there, too. He adopted a stray dog that hung around the station, named him "Gas," and brought him to every rehearsal. I was worried about the poor dog's ears, but Gas didn't seem to mind.

Javier had a beat-up blue station wagon, so Heart Attack had wheels now. And somebody old enough to drive. We played an empty club way out in Dover, New Jersey on a Tuesday night and an all-ages matinee on the Upper East Side.

Javier lived at the Kenmore—a rat-infested hotel on 23rd Street that literally smelled like shit—in a room barely large enough for his single bed. The Kenmore was dangerous, crammed with lunatics and junkies living on disability checks and government assistance. The guy across the hall from Javier never left his room. Ever. The hotel staff went in there and changed his sheets once a month. You could smell him. It was frightening.

Javier and I hung out all over downtown. If I was too tired to make it back to Queens, I'd crash on his concrete floor with my head under his dirty little sink.

One fall day, as Javier and I were hustling across Cooper Square in our overcoats, he ran over to the huge black-cube sculpture in the middle of Astor Place and shouted, "Max! Let's give this theeng a spin." (I have no idea why he started calling me "Max" at some point along the way.)

We pushed and grunted with all our might, but we could barely budge it. Some stranger jumped in, and the three of us got the cube spinning slowly. A rite of passage.

I got Heart Attack another Monday-night audition at CBGB. Onstage, I cut my arm with my knife. I thought that would be cool, but the booker was not amused.

"Fuck it," Javier said, "everybody wanna be the Wash Brains, Max." That's what he called the Bad Brains. He said they had brainwashed the scene into following them. "Let's do a real tour—in Mexico City," he added. "I can set it up with my people."

Brandon's mom said okay right away. I think she wanted some alone time with her new husband.

"No way!" my mother exclaimed. "You're in junior high. You are not going to Mexico."

I came home from school every day and went straight to

bed. I just lay there, pretending to sleep. I wouldn't come out to eat or anything.

After a week of my Sleeping Beauty routine, my mother caved. She met Javier, who promised to take care of me.

Brandon, Javier, and I flew down to Mexico City. We were booked for two weeks, six shows a week, at the Hip Setenta club. It had a big stage and a nice balcony. We stayed with Javier's parents and rehearsed in their backyard, while children and chickens ran all over the street. Javier's girlfriend, Dali, came over to hang out. I was amazed that I could buy liquor at the corner store without an ID.

I got to work on a flier at the kitchen table with my glue stick and a newspaper. The National Rifle Association was on the rise and guns were on my mind. When John Lennon was shot, Javier had dragged me all the way from Whitestone to the Dakota, Lennon's grand apartment building overlooking Central Park. We stood outside for hours with hundreds of crying people on that dark December night. I bitched the whole time that Lennon was a rich hippie, but looking back, I'm glad I was there.

Our B-movie actor/president Ronald Reagan was shot by another nut with a gun three months later. Even the pope was getting threats. Nobody was safe, it seemed.

I cut out pictures of the pope and a gun. I glued these onto my flier, with the gun pointing at the pope. We pasted copies around Hip Setenta's neighborhood. This did not go over well in heavily Catholic Mexico City. During our first sound check, a man showed up drunk and enraged, threatening to kill us because we had "put a gun to *el papa*!" On his way out the door, he yelled, "I'm gonna come back tonight and shoot you!"

"I'm not scared," I said to Javier. "We're gonna play anyway."

Javier nodded. Brandon looked spooked, but he nodded too.

During our show, I kept one eye on the balcony, in case an angry Mexican leaped onto the stage like John Wilkes Booth. The crowd was pretty crazy, dancing and yelling. They kept wanting more. We ran out of our own songs and had to dig up some covers. It was like that for all six nights. The fingernails on my right hand got so worn down that I was bleeding all over my guitar.

One night, Brandon grabbed his mic while holding onto his bass. A big shock sent him flying across the stage—and he was a chunky kid. Brandon was shaken up, but okay.

We didn't get shot, but during our encore one night, a rail-thin guy in leather pants and wraparound sunglasses jumped onstage, smashing bottles and rolling around in the glass. He was Illy Bleeding, lead singer for the Mexican punk band Size. After the show, he regaled us with crazy stories, like the time he was beaten up and thrown down the stairs at Max's for being gay.

As we chatted, a sexy girl floated my way in a cloud of strong perfume. Her name was Lula. She had Bettie Page hair and was wearing fishnet stockings, a tight vinyl skirt, black eyeliner, and lots of red lipstick. She was older than me and came on really strong. I was excited, but nervous. I wanted sex, but that bad experience with Jade Shira still haunted me.

Lula pulled me close, put a pill in my mouth, and kissed me. I spit it on the floor when she wasn't looking, like R.P. McMurphy in *Cuckoo's Nest*. Then we fooled around a little in the dressing room.

Heart Attack was written up in local papers and magazines. We even played on TV. I was feeling like quite the rock star when I met Dali's cute sister, Patty. We spent an afternoon drinking a bottle of cheap bourbon and listening to records. I got so wasted that I forgot I had a show that night. By the time sound check rolled around, I was puking and couldn't get off the couch. Javier ran to the pharmacy and came back with some vitamin B that was cut with some kinda speed.

Within minutes, I was up and ready to go. And impressed with what you could get over the counter in Mexico.

Chapter 12

University of the Streets

Finding peace in a local riot
—"Before You Go"

Mexico City got me even more fired up about making music my life. Getting on a plane with my guitar and traveling somewhere exciting and new with my friends was a great feeling. I wanted more.

But back in New York, I needed to find somewhere Heart Attack could play a lot and build a crowd.

I didn't *go west, young man*, like the pioneers of old. I walked east along St. Marks, following homemade posters advertising five-dollar shows at some place called A7 on the Lower East Side.

The fliers were wheat-pasted onto lampposts, mailboxes, and the plywood walls around construction sites. They led me—and other punk kids—to a grungy bar on the corner of 7th Street and Avenue A.

A7 was an illegal after-hours spot right across from Tompkins Square Park. Anyone who ventured into Tompkins after dark risked getting mugged . . . or worse. Junkies and unhoused people sprawled on splintered benches, and passed out on patchy lawns under beat-up elms that were barely hanging on. Even the trees were down-and-out.

A7 stayed open long after the bars closed at four a.m. Sketchy characters doing the cocaine crawl rolled in to cop and keep drinking, well into the next day. But in the tiny back room, tough young bands like the Mad, Stimulators, and False Prophets were tearing it up. Stimulators bassist Nick Marden painted three words on the back of his leather jacket that said it all:

LOUD
FAST
RULES!

This was where Heart Attack could find a gig—if we didn't get murdered.

I started spending every weekend at A7 in 1981. My mother let me go because she knew it was about the music for me—not drugs. On Friday and Saturday nights, I danced myself into a sweaty, soaking mess with a bunch of new friends until six a.m. Steam rose off our heads when we stepped outside into the frigid predawn air.

Getting home took me forever because the subway made every local stop at that hour. Sometimes I'd doze off on the train and be jolted awake by a transit cop banging his club on the metal railing, right near my face. I'd finally get out of the subway at Flushing–Main Street, where I would wait for the Q15 bus to Whitestone, which ran just once an hour.

Exhausted, I'd lean against the bus stop wearing my old-man raincoat over my leather jacket. Creepy guys cruised by extra slow in their cars. I nervously ignored their stares until they finally moved on.

Unwanted attention from chickenhawks came at me—and probably a lot of boys wandering around New York after midnight—all the time. And pay phones rang all over the city. This mystified me.

One night, out of curiosity, I picked up a ringing pay phone and held the receiver to my ear. A man's voice commanded, "Look up." I did, and there he was, shirtless and unzipped, pressed against his apartment window whacking off. "You wanna come up?" he groaned. I hung up real fast.

The Lower East Side was dangerous back then, rife with drug-dealing gangs fighting turf wars over every corner and shooting gallery. The saying was: *Avenue A—adventurous. Avenue B—bold, Avenue C—crazy. And if you get to Avenue D—you're dead.*

In between shootouts and stabbings, ordinary working-class people—Puerto Ricans, Dominicans, African Americans, Poles, Ukrainians—did their best to go about their lives and raise their families. Some buildings were so run-down that children got lead poisoning from eating scraps of peeling paint nicknamed "Avenue D potato chips."

The locals weren't too happy about the rambunctious white kids with mohawks and combat boots infiltrating their neighborhood. I had empty bottles thrown at my head more than once, followed by Spanish curses, while walking down Avenue A. Two Puerto Rican kids mugged me at knifepoint one afternoon for six bucks, right in front of the Boys' Club of New York on 10th and A.

I loved the Lower East Side anyway for pierogis at Odessa, thirty-cent egg creams at Ray's Candy Store, greasy dollar pizza slices at Stromboli—and A7. Even though bands didn't start playing until well after midnight, that back room was always packed with kids like me willing to dodge a little danger to find a place that felt like home, and friends who felt like family.

We shared a disdain for hippies—of course. But also for those older punks who had self-destructed. "Too Much Junkie Business," like the Heartbreakers sang. No thanks. Dope was scary—and everywhere. It was killing my heroes, and I didn't want any part of it. Besides, I hated needles. They hurt.

A friend told me heroin withdrawal was like the worst flu you ever had, times ten. That didn't sound fun to me. Even one hit of weed rendered me useless. I couldn't play music high. I was more likely to try to take my pants off over my head and pass out. I preferred racing around hopped up on adrenaline and testosterone.

A rehearsal studio called 171-A on Avenue A and 10th Street started throwing shows, too. Now there were even more hardcore gigs every weekend. None of these shows were advertised in the *Village Voice*. You had to run into somebody on St. Marks, or see a flier at the Rat Cage—a makeshift basement record store on Avenue A. The entrance was a metal cellar door on the sidewalk. Dave Rat Cage and his wife, Cathy, lived down there, behind a hanging bedsheet near the boilers. Dave and Cathy let us kids get warm in their place before the clubs opened. We'd hang out listening to the new records Dave wrote about in his newsprint fanzine, *Mouth of the Rat*.

Beat poet Allen Ginsberg lived in the neighborhood, and somehow I got his phone number. My friends and I would crank-call him from a pay phone on Avenue B, saying sexy things in our teenage voices. Allen would respond gently, "Oh? Where did I meet you? Down at the pier?" We'd laugh and hang up.

I'd see legendary characters like Ginsberg, Taylor Mead, and white-haired dandy Quentin Crisp in his velvet jackets roaming around. They seemed like relics from another time to me. Looking back, I wish I had appreciated them more.

When my mother landed a two-bedroom apartment in our building, I finally got my own room. She turned the breakfast nook off the kitchen into a little room for Juliet.

I loved the smell of fresh paint that hit me the first time

I walked into that apartment. To this day, the smell of fresh paint feels like success to me—like anything is possible.

My mother was not thrilled, however, that I was sleeping away my Saturdays and Sundays recovering from all-nighters. She would bang her vacuum against my bedroom door, yelling, "These eggs are getting cold!" But those nights on the Lower East Side were fast becoming everything to me.

My mother liked to say, "Show me who your friends are, and I'll show you who you are." I felt good about my new friends, like I had found my tribe. I felt hugely inspired, as if some creative door had been unlocked in my brain. I wrote a storm of new songs that were harder, faster, more aggressive—and even shorter. I channeled all my angst into them—from being picked on at school to hating all those kids who couldn't accept anyone who didn't look exactly like them. And I had my band—but I didn't know how to get us to the next level.

"We need a manager, Max," Javier said.

I had just the right lunatic in mind.

Mojo was nearly seven feet tall. He was one of the few Black punks on the scene besides the Bad Brains and Raven—the short tuxedo-wearing sax player for the Stimulators. Mojo worked the door at Berlin, a second-story after-hours club on lower Broadway. Sometimes he stood at the top of Berlin's steep stairs with his arms crossed, looking very intimidating. But mostly he lounged against the wall. I met him when the Undead—one of my favorite bands—played at Studio 10, the yippie headquarters on Bleecker Street.

I was psyched to go see the Undead. They were the perfect punk power trio, led by former Misfits guitarist Bobby Steele. Bobby was twenty-five, pale, and thin, with big blue eyes rimmed with black eyeliner and short jet-black hair. He lived in black spandex pants that clung to his skinny legs, and white high-top sneakers. Bobby wore a leather jacket over his bare bony chest. He walked with a black cane because he'd had polio as a child, but he wasn't afraid to swing it in a fight.

Bobby loved the Beatles and wrote really catchy songs. Unfortunately, when he ran into John Lennon outside the Mudd Club one night, Bobby was so drunk that he puked all over his hero's shoes. He lived on East 4th Street with some pet snakes and rats that he was always happy to show me and my friends. He was a sweet guy who enjoyed telling us stories and sharing pointers on how to get a gig. But he also had a taste for trouble.

Bobby got his sneakers from his crazy girlfriend Lucy, whose father owned a major shoe company. She was a thin, angry blonde who did lots of drugs and was always screaming and starting fights. Wherever Lucy went, she was guaranteed to cause a scene. This made for lots of trouble at Undead shows. Fights broke out often, instigated by Lucy and amped up by the Undead posse—wild guys like Joe Nails, Ira Asher, Richie, and Gigo.

The calm inside the Undead storm was drummer Patrick Blanck. Patrick was a very tall, soft-spoken vegetarian who loved animals and rockabilly. At thirty, he seemed old to me, but I loved hanging out with him. He told me once that he had been a kept man. I didn't know what that meant, but something else Patrick said really stuck with me. He told me that when someone asked Louis Armstrong to define jazz, Armstrong replied, "If you have to ask, you'll never know."

"Punk is like that," Patrick said.

Sometimes, though, older guys told me things that weren't so poetic.

Ira Asher looked like a punk-rock Jackie Gleason. He was a loudmouthed, roly-poly Undead fan with big round eyes, a padlocked chain around his neck, and safety pins through his ears. Ira talked real tough, but he was a softie at heart who melted around little babies, and kissed any dog he came across on the street. He loved to eat his matzo brei at Kiev, a Ukrainian diner on Second Avenue. "They make it just like my mutha!" he would say. But at gigs, Ira was ready to pull the chains off his boots and fight anyone who fucked with his friends.

One afternoon, Ira invited me to hang out with him and his equally rotund girlfriend, Robin, at their place on Norfolk Street. We listened to records in the living room, and I felt so cool sitting there drinking a Budweiser tallboy. Then Ira said, "Hey Jesse, come here," and walked me into their bedroom. Scary rawhide whips and leather crops hung all over the walls. Chains and cuffs were hanging from the walls, too. "This is what you're gonna get into when you grow up," he declared, gesturing proudly at his mini dungeon.

"Uh . . . really?" I said, but what I was thinking was: *This is clearly your trip, buddy.* It was tough for me to walk back into the living room, see Robin, and keep a straight face. My only question was, who chained up who? I figured she probably beat his ass.

Studio 10 was just a block from CBGB. The yippies always had free pot, too. Unfortunately, our scene didn't always respect their hospitality.

The Undead were on fire that night at Studio 10. Their crowd got all riled up—and punks have to fuck with hippies, right? We started smashing beer bottles on the floor, knocking over chairs, and going wild. The yippies got mad and tried to stop the show. They threatened to call the cops, which we found so hypocritical that we really went nuts. Mojo dove onto Studio 10's plywood bar screaming, "Fuck you, hippies and yippies!" and knocking every bottle to the floor. Raven—

that little penguin—was screeching, "Stop it, Mojo! Stop it now!" A small riot broke out—par for the course at an Undead show. The yippies chased us out of their club and down Bleecker Street, where we escaped into the subway.

Naturally, I was thrilled by all this action. I felt like we were these bad kids making some real trouble.

After that, I kept seeing Mojo around. I mean, you couldn't miss the guy.

So, late one night, Javier and I climbed those steep stairs to Berlin and asked Mojo, "Will you be our manager?"

"All right," he shrugged.

Papa Joe, born in Kyiv, fighting in the tsar's army.

Papa Artie and my mother as a baby while he was still in the service.

My parents, Enid and Paul Malin, on their wedding night.

My mom in a photo from college.

My mom reading to me in Whitestone, Queens, while I sit there with my eye patch and glasses.

Papa Artie, cousin Matt, and me.

My dad with me and Juliet in his apartment on Second Avenue in Manhattan.

With my sister Juliet near the East River. I was a Cub Scout for ten minutes. We had meetings in the basement of Whitestone Hospital.

Lost in the supermarket. It's my first leather jacket— that actually was vinyl, but I thought it was cool. Just goofing around in the local Waldbaum's on 154th Street in Whitestone. Holding up some aftershave, but I'm still too young to shave or know.

In my kitchen on Grand Street just before I moved to Los Angeles for a short time.

Kyra Kverno

Laura Levine

The first day I met Jimmy G., on St. Marks Place outside of Paul McGregor's BC Club (the Before Club). This was before hardcore matinees were a thing. Just two Queens guys making trouble in the city.

Heart Attack's first gig at CBGB on the Monday audition night . . . We failed.

Coney Island High, 15 St. Marks Place. It wasn't a high school and it wasn't in Brooklyn.

Heart Attack playing Max's Kansas City, July 15, 1980.

Right and below: Heart Attack—me, Javier Madariaga, and John Frawley—on E. 12th Street, August 1981.

Heart Attack at Rock Against Racism in Central Park, 1984.

Me and Holly Ramos, 1985.

Above: My business card. "Anytime, anywhere." *Left:* Driving my Econoline van in Queens, 1987. Van man with a plan, or in this case, a sad man with a van.

Giorgio Gomelsky in his loft in Chelsea. "I'm up on 24th Street and I'm looking at a life."

With Holly Ramos, recovering after I rolled the van on Route 80 and totaled it in 1986.

D Generation, Madison Square Garden, July 1996.

Hope—me, Michael Wildwood, Danny Sage, and John Carco—on the steps of the *Taxi Driver* building on E. 13th Street.

D Generation—Michael Wildwood, Danny Sage, and manager Jon Goldwater—signing our Columbia Records contract in the dressing room at CBGB, 1995.

Marti Wilkerson, the sixth member of D Generation.

D Generation—Michael Wildwood, me, Danny Sage, Rick Bacchus, and Howie Pyro—at the Continental, 5 a.m., 1992.

With Howie Pyro at the "Lucky Monkey" party at Don Hill's, 1997.

Jack Flanagan in Hollywood.

Bellvue—Joe Rizzo, Esko Poldvere, me, and Johnny Pisano.

Dave Szekart

A note for a loan from Joey Ramone.

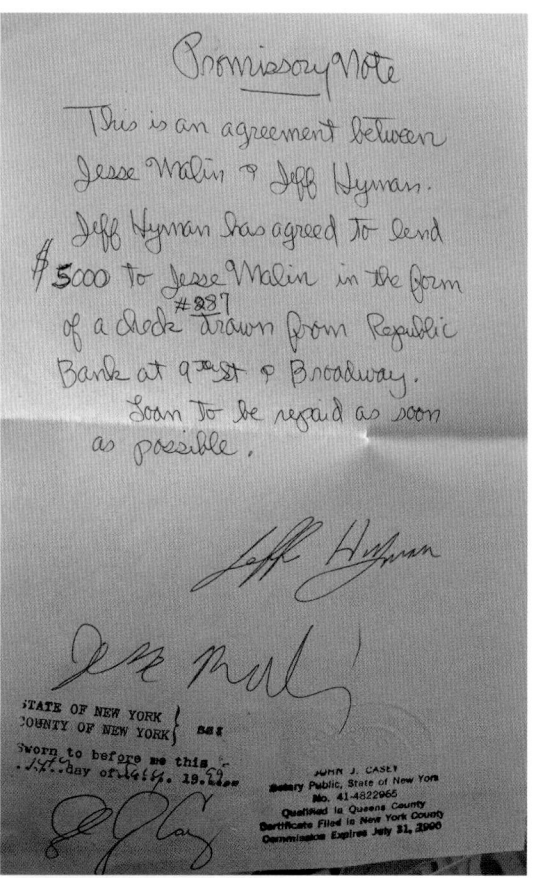

With Joey Ramone and Jeremy Chatzky at Ronnie Spector's holiday party, December 2000.

With H.R. (from Bad Brains) on the last night of the Continental, December 15, 2018.

At the video shoot for "Queen of the Underworld," 2003.

With Billie Joe Armstrong of Green Day.

With Bruce Springsteen on the set for the "Broken Radio" video.

Bob Gruen

Danny Clinch

Glitter in the Gutter promo shot, in the basement of HiFi Bar.

Chapter 13

Don't Tell Your Sister

*When it all goes down on a corner
In a sad and beautiful world*
—"Oh Sheena"

As Heart Attack's manager, Mojo booked us exactly one gig—at A7. He called my house to tell me, and didn't say hello when my mother answered. Just demanded to speak to me. She handed me the phone and whispered, "Who is this fucking guy?"

Luckily, the booker at Max's Kansas City, Peter Crowley, took a liking to me. Peter brought me into his office and let me sit at his desk and use the phone to call up bands and book some shows. The first show I booked was Heart Attack with Reagan Youth, Even Worse, and Kraut. A hundred people showed up. They knocked over all the tables—that's how you knew it was a good night at Max's.

Mojo jumped onstage during Heart Attack's set. He grabbed a mic and screamed, "Ant people take off your war paint!" in a British accent, over and over. I spent the rest of our show trying to shove my gigantic new manager off the stage.

After our set, I went outside to get some air. As I stood on the sidewalk with Mojo, blood streamed from a cut over my eye where I'd gotten hit with a mic stand. I couldn't get it to stop. Some girl tugged on Mojo's sleeve. "Your friend's bleeding," she said. "You better take him to the hospital."

"I'm his manager!" Mojo bellowed, yanking his arm out of her grasp. "Don't tell me what to do!" He wandered off, and left me on the sidewalk.

When the show was over and the money had been counted, Peter handed me a wad of cash. "Put this in your underwear before you get on the train," he said

That show got a write-up in the British magazine *Sounds*. Heart Attack was photographed for it in a burnt-out building on Avenue C. I felt a bit awkward in front of the camera, but the pictures came out pretty badass.

Whether you loved or hated him, Mojo was quite the presence. The Beastie Boys wrote their song "Egg Raid on Mojo" about the night they pelted him with eggs. At least he got Heart Attack into A7. It was a dump, but it was a dump where we could play whenever we wanted.

The Mob played A7 too. Jack and I were still rivals, but I had to give it up to the Mob. They were one of the fastest, tightest bands around. Even when they went on at six in the morning, they killed it. I don't know how they brought it like that after smoking weed in the Toronado on Avenue A all night.

I got my revenge when I poached the Mob's bass player, John Frawley, a construction worker's son from Flushing. When I met him, he had long hair and wore a denim jacket that said: *Rolling Stones—The First Punks*. As he got more into hardcore, he tossed the jacket, shaved his head, and donned a black wool cap. Frawley was seventeen when he joined Heart Attack after Brandon left. That was my favorite lineup: me, John, and Javier.

Frawley and I were troublemakers. We'd run down the street kicking over garbage cans and screaming at the top of our lungs. We'd swing by Kiev after an all-nighter, spread our cheeks, and press our naked asses up against the window while people ate their borscht and challah. What can I say? *Animal House* was still our favorite movie.

I couldn't wait for Friday nights, when Heart Attack rehearsed at New Wave Sound in Flushing. One hour cost fifteen dollars, five bucks per person. We rehearsed hard, with no wasted time. I wanted us super tight, able to blast from one song into the next.

After rehearsal, if we needed cash—and we always needed cash—we hopped three trains and got out at Astor Place. We walked down St. Marks—Frawley and I lugging big black guitar cases; Javier with nothing but a pair of drumsticks in his back pocket. We'd stop to tell our friends hanging out in front of Trash and Vaudeville, and on stoops along the way, that we were playing that night.

When we reached A7, I'd hunt down Dave Gibson, who ran the place and sold coke out of a Noxzema jar. Dave would scrawl HEART ATTACK with a Sharpie on his list of a half dozen bands that were going to play, and tape it on the side door. John, Javier, and I would hang out for hours—drinking on the street, goofing on passersby, and dancing to the other bands—until it was our turn.

A cheap drum kit and amps were nailed to the tiny wooden stage, which rose just a couple inches from the floor. The amps were blown and the bass drum head was a piece of cardboard cut out of a pizza box from Sal's next door. If a mosh pit erupted during our set, we considered it a success. Dave paid two hundred bucks, which was a lot of money to us back then.

In 1981, the Bad Brains moved to New York after being banned from every club in DC. They lived together at 171-A. Sometimes I'd be walking down Avenue A and H.R. would pop out of a doorway wearing an overcoat with a Star of David armband. His hair was longer now, twisted into dreads.

Wielding a Bible, he'd grab my hand tightly, proclaiming: "Rastafari! Selassie! King of Kings. Praise the twelve tribes of Israel!"

"Hey, H.R., good to see you," I'd say, thrilled to be talking to my hero but confused by the Bible. What the heck was he talking about? I'd been trying to get away from this religious stuff my whole life.

But H.R. would look me in the eyes and smile so warmly that it made me feel really good. He'd press his fist to his heart, repeating, "One love, true love," with great sincerity. H.R. was so positive and passionate that you couldn't help but want to be in his presence. So I would nod my head and listen respectfully, because he was the greatest front man I had ever seen.

Also, the Bad Brains had the best amps, and a Lucite drum kit that sounded like thunder. They were very generous about letting opening bands use their gear. If Heart Attack ever got the chance, I just knew we'd blow everyone away.

That Christmas, the Bad Brains played A7 on those beat-up amps and busted drums. A hundred people jammed into a room that held maybe forty. H.R.'s performance was so intense that his fist went right through the drop ceiling. The floor was a sweaty, swirling pit of bodies—fists and boots flying. And the Bad Brains sounded just as magnificent and powerful as they did at CBGB.

If I spotted another punk on the 7 train on my rides into the city, I'd give him a nod. We might start talking—maybe even plan to ride home to Queens later that night and have each other's backs.

Fights broke out on the train all the time, especially late at night. Metalheads hated punks. Punks hated hippies. Rappers hated all us dumb white kids. Mix in a few subway slashers, raving drunks, and pissed-off transit cops, and it didn't make for the smoothest ride.

I had one punk friend in Whitestone, Anthony Ferrante. We shaved each other's heads in my bathroom and sped around on our bikes blasting mixtapes on our Sony Walkmans. Anthony's grandmother only had one leg, and didn't speak much English. When we'd raid the fridge in his kitchen, she'd wheel around us yelling, "Disgust! Disgust!" in her thick Italian accent.

I met Lyle Hysen through an ad for a singer in *Good Times*. I took the bus out to Great Neck, Long Island and walked up the winding road to Lyle's nice house. He was a soft-spoken, nerdy keyboardist with curly brown hair and pale white skin. We banged out some punk covers in the basement with his drummer—another hyperactive little guy named Danny Sage.

"Hey, at least this guy sings in key better than our last guy," Lyle said to Danny.

After that day, Lyle and I spoke on the phone every night like clockwork, turning each other on to new bands and brainstorming about places where we could gig. Lyle even started a fanzine called *Damaged Goods* to spread the word about this new scene.

That June of 1981, I teamed up with my frenemy Jack Flanagan to put on a two-night "Punk Comes to Queens" festival at Shamus Pub. We promised the owners that we would pack the place all weekend with heavy drinkers. They believed our underage asses for some reason. We put up fliers all over town: *Punk Comes to Queens—Bring Your Own Towel!*

The only two bands we actually managed to book were the Mob and Heart Attack. Our turnout wasn't great, but our audience did buy lots of booze. Unfortunately, it was from the deli across the street, and they drank it in the parking lot.

I made two more friends for life that weekend: John Rizzo and John Carco. Rizzo was taller than everybody else, and could outdrink anyone. He was from a beaten-down neighborhood in Brooklyn called Bushwick. Rizzo had bad skin, but was still a good-looking guy with his strong jaw and thick brown hair. He wore a black T-shirt, jeans, and white suspenders with a Clash badge pinned to them.

Rizzo jumped onstage uninvited while Heart Attack was playing and started singing "White Riot" by the Clash, drunk out of his mind. His frantic energy grabbed everybody's attention, so we went with it. Rizz wound up in the parking lot puking his guts out, but then he was back for round two.

Carco was a tall, scrawny kid with long black hair. He wore a skull-and-crossbones bolo tie that said *Death or Glory*. He looked like a Ramone, but also kind of soft and androgynous, like a seventies rock star.

Rizzo, Carco, and Lyle became fast friends that weekend, too, and formed a band called the Misguided. So, yeah, Punk Comes to Queens didn't pack the place, but it brought a lot of people together, and that made me happy.

Years later, whenever I'd run into Ralphie, I'd say, "Remember Shamus Pub?"

"Yo, man, I passed by there the other day and that place is *still* shaking!" Ralphie always replied.

Out of that weekend came more friends than I'd ever had. Friends who became family—there for each other through thick and thin: from fun road trips to car crashes, from no money to big record deals, from deaths that gutted us to good times that lifted us up again.

We truly were from Planet Queens. We met up at the Clam Bar on Roosevelt and Main, a little dive that served cheap drinks to men who sat silently on barstools, sunk in their thoughts. You'd click a quarter and dime on the bar, and the grizzled bartender would pour a five-inch glass of beer. We'd have a few drinks and plan our next move.

Javier, Frawley, and I dropped into the Clam Bar regularly after rehearsals. We'd meet Carco, Rizzo, Lyle, and Danny there, too, and get our buzz going before hopping on the 7 train.

The old-timers didn't seem to mind us. We wore old-man shirts after all, and went to the same barber shops to get our hair clipped for three bucks. We felt a connection to those men. There was something real about drinking in a dark bar with them.

One night, we met up at the Clam Bar and went to see the Dead Boys at the Playroom on 9th Street and Sixth Avenue. We still loved that seventies punk rock. But it was a terrible gig. Cheetah Chrome broke a string and was a fucked-up mess. And I drank more than I ever had in my life.

As my friends and I were walking back to the subway, we passed a fruit stand. I grabbed a bin of oranges and dumped them all over the sidewalk. Then we trashed it all. We pulled down more bins, kicking and smashing fruit all over the sidewalk. The owner came out shouting and we ran like the devil was after us.

It was a thrill, like the Studio 10 riot. But even in my wasted state, I knew all we did was hurt some hardworking guy. You could hear it in his voice. I felt ashamed. We were being knuckleheads from Queens—even though we thought we were better.

I passed out on the L train and rode it back and forth in a stupor between Brooklyn and Manhattan. The truth was, I had gotten so drunk because I was really upset about something. Too upset to talk about it, even with my friends.

I had been working all summer at the gas station to save up enough money to buy a real Gibson SG guitar. My boss was a big fat guy named Eddie who was so hairy that he had to shave his face up to his eyeballs. He lived in a trailer behind the station with his German shepherd, and smelled pretty foul. He paid me in cash, which I socked away in my bedroom dresser. It was adding up, and I could feel my dream about to finally come true.

My mother was managing a makeup store at Queens Center Mall. We left together every morning so she could drop me at the gas station. Somebody must have spotted our routine. I came home one evening and the door to our apartment was unlocked. I ran to my bedroom and frantically searched my dresser. All my money was gone. Worse, when my mother checked on her wedding china and silver, they were gone too. We suspected an inside job—maybe a worker who didn't have to break into the building, just into our apartment.

"Please don't tell Juliet," my mother said. "She'll be too scared."

I was devastated, so I did what I heard you're supposed to do when bad things happen: go out and drink away the pain.

As morning commuters swarmed onto the L train, I came to, and got my sick self over to the 7 train. It was so hot outside that when I finally made it home, I sprawled out on the linoleum in the kitchen. Eventually, I dragged myself off the floor and to the refrigerator. I grabbed a quart of cold orange juice, drank it all down, and puked like I never had before.

This put me on the straight edge path for some time. And taught me my first lesson about drinking when you're down and out: it just pours gasoline on the fire.

That robbery stuck with me for a long time. It felt so personal, and I had worked so hard.

Chapter 14

Misfits at the Ritz

The place is packed
And the kids are jacked
On those antisocial songs
—"Turn Up the Mains"

I hated junior high. My teachers were still mad that I had skipped three weeks of school to go to Mexico City with Heart Attack. I never got caught up on my homework either, because I spent my nights rehearsing and running around to shows. It didn't help that I came back from Mexico wearing lots of messy black eyeliner and acting totally disinterested in anything they tried to teach me.

My teachers were fed up with my clowning around. Before I left, I had been in a gifted class that would have let me skip a grade and graduate a year early. Now they were threatening to pull me out of it. The thought of having to do that extra year of school made me sick.

Other students picked fights with me all the time. I was quick to fight back, so I was hauled into the principal's office pretty often. I spent lots of time sitting in detention bored out of my mind. I've got to be honest, though. Back in grade school, I had been the one picking fights with other kids. I thought I was a tough guy, and I had a lot of anger inside after my parents divorced.

I got into a lot of fights until I ran into boys—mostly Italian kids—with older brothers and fathers who beat them. Those kids getting their asses kicked at home had a higher tolerance for pain. They were tougher than me. I started losing, so I quit picking fights.

My mother hit me sometimes, but not too much—and never very hard. My father wasn't around enough to hit me, but he did notice that I was pretty angry and always doing my kung fu moves. He made one thing very clear: "Jesse, whatever you do, you never hit a girl."

Getting into music helped me a lot. Playing in a band and dancing at shows were better outlets for my pent-up rage. By junior high, I wasn't picking fights anymore. But I did fight back when pushed too far.

A snobby group of girls in designer jeans and feathered disco hair made fun of me every day in Spanish class.

"Ewww, you're so gross! What are all those stupid buttons on your jacket?"

"Ooooh, you finally cut that nasty hair. What a dumb haircut! You're such a loser."

This went on for weeks. I felt so humiliated and embarrassed. I couldn't take it anymore, but I didn't know what to do. After all, my father had told me to never hit a girl. I really wanted to shut them up somehow. So, one day I walked over to the ringleader, pulled out my penis, and slapped it on her desk a few times. She shrieked. The teacher ran over, grabbed me by the arm, and dragged me down to the principal's office. I barely had a chance to zip up.

Let me say—before anybody gets it twisted—that I don't condone my juvenile behavior. At the time, though, I took a certain glee in rendering my tormentors completely hysterical.

Principal Pittman was not amused. He called my mother to come get me, and told her what I did. "This young man could be a potential rapist! Look how he's dressed!" he exclaimed, pointing at my beat-up combat boots and ripped

T-shirt. "This outlandish outfit is not appropriate for my school."

"He really is a good kid," my mother insisted. "He just dresses like that because he likes the punk rock. You know, the Circle Jerk, the Dead Kennedy, the Black Flags . . ." Her voice trailed off as she realized she probably wasn't helping my case.

Turning on me, Mr. Pittman demanded, "Do you know what they do to radicals like you in this country?"

I shrugged.

"The Abbie Hoffmans? The Charlie Mansons?" he raved.

I rolled my eyes. "What?"

"No school for two weeks!"

Wow, I thought, *this is great*. But as soon as we got in the car, my mother snapped.

"You are grounded for a month, young man. No TV! No telephone! Absolutely no guitar! I don't want to see you set one foot outside your room."

That night, my mother's boyfriend came over. Frank was heavily into horse racing. In fact, after hearing about my Mexican adventures, he took me aside and asked if we could fly back down to Mexico and pick up some of those special "vitamins." He wanted to slip them to a horse or two.

Through our thin walls, I thought I heard my name, so I tiptoed into the hall to eavesdrop.

"You would not *believe* what my son did at school today," my mother was saying.

"What," Frank grunted, clearly disinterested.

"He took out his penis and slapped it on a girl's desk!"

Instantly, Frank cracked up. Then my mother cracked up. After that, I wasn't grounded anymore.

This was a big relief to me, because Heart Attack was about

to make its first record. But first we had to make some demos.

I used our A7 cash to book a few hours at Roxy Studios, which was in a warehouse in a spooky, desolate part of Long Island City. It was right off the 7 train, though, so that worked for us.

Mojo came out to supervise the session, which started at noon. But Mojo had been up all night working the door at Berlin. He fell asleep on the control-room couch, snoring away while we recorded eight songs. Somehow, though, Mojo wound up with the tapes. I didn't see them again for twenty-five years.

Frawley, Javier, and I returned to Roxy Studios a few weeks later to record three songs for real. Lyle Hysen released *God Is Dead* on his Damaged Goods label in September 1981.

God Is Dead may have been the first New York hardcore record. It sold out fast after Tim Sommer played it a bunch on his WNYU radio program *Noise the Show*. Every hardcore kid in the tristate area listened to Tim's show on Tuesday nights.

I got an earful from Bleecker Bob: "How come I never got the Heart Attack record? That anti-Semite down the block got copies!" He was bitching about Ed Bahlman from 99 Records, who I'm pretty sure was Jewish.

Tim even interviewed me and Frawley on his show. Javier refused to go. "I am a Mexican drummer," he declared. "I don't do no radio. I don't do no benefits. I don't do nothing unless I get paid."

About a month later, Tim called me and asked if Heart Attack would like to open for the Misfits at the Ritz. The Ritz was the biggest, hottest new nightclub downtown. It held 1,500 people and booked acts like Tina Turner and U2.

On off nights, the Ritz was a cool dance club that

played new wave and goth. My friends and I hung out there sometimes—drinking, trying to pick up girls, and watching these new things called "music videos" on the thirty-foot screen above the stage. Being at the Ritz felt like living in the future.

One night, I was there with Carco and Rizzo. As soon as Rizz had a couple beers in him, he was off on a mission to hook up. Pretty soon, though, he circled back to me and Carco, looking spooked.

"What's up?" I shouted over "Pretty in Pink" by the Psychedelic Furs.

"Man, so freaking weird!" Rizzo yelled back. "This little guy in, like, his thirties comes up to me, looks me up and down, and says, 'You can have any girl you want in the club tonight to fuck. But while you're fucking her, I'm going to be fucking you in the ass.'"

"Holy shit!" I responded, laughing. Carco burst out laughing, too.

"So I said to the guy," Rizzo continued, "'Who the fuck do you think you are?' And he says, 'You ever seen that movie *Dog Day Afternoon?*' And I said, 'Yeah, so what?' And he says, 'I'm the motherfucking guy it's about, that's what.'"

"No fucking way!" I yelled.

Rizzo shrugged. "Who the hell knows?"

Years later, I learned that after John Wojtowicz got out of prison in 1978 for that bank robbery, he hung out at the Ritz.

Hell yeah, I wanted to open for the Misfits there.

Somehow the Undead wound up on the bill, too, even though Bobby Steele had bad blood with the Misfits ever since he was kicked out of the band in 1979.

What could possibly go wrong?

The Misfits were bodybuilding beasts who played horror

punk in skull-face makeup. They twisted their bangs into long devil locks and tromped around menacingly in leather outfits and motorcycle boots—almost like a punk-rock version of KISS.

The Misfits had great, catchy songs—kinda like if Elvis met the Ramones on Halloween in New Jersey. I thought their act was a little corny, but I was still very excited to open for them. However, Heart Attack was going to need better gear for that huge stage. I borrowed a bass amp the size of a fridge from Andy Apathy. He played bass in Reagan Youth, a popular local band from Forest Hills, where the Ramones grew up.

Before I ever saw Reagan Youth play, I met a shrimpy kid named Steve Poss at A7. He wore jeans, sneakers, and a red marching-band jacket with *DEAD KENNEDYS* painted on the back. He had a funny high-pitched nasal voice with a thick Queens accent. Everybody called him Poss.

"What are you up to?" I asked him.

"I bark for Reagan Youth!" Poss squeaked proudly.

I figured that meant he handed out fliers and talked up their shows on the street.

When I went to see Reagan Youth, I was startled to see Poss push through the crowd, climb onstage, and start barking into a mic like a chihuahua for their song "In Dog We Trust."

Frawley was psyched to play through Andy's giant bass amp, and Lyle loaned Javier his Ludwig drum kit. Carco came to help out, and we shoved all the gear into Javier's station wagon and drove to the Ritz.

The Misfits pulled up on a huge flatbed truck loaded with massive amps. They looked like a football team walking into the Ritz with their entourage of beefy dudes.

Backstage, about to go on, I felt unbelievably amped up.

When we got the signal, I walked out reading the *New York Post*. I paced around the stage until Javier counted us in. Then I furiously ripped up the newspaper and we slammed into one of the best sets Heart Attack ever played. The Ritz had roped off a small area on the floor for people who wanted to "slam dance." That got demolished in about thirty seconds.

The Undead played a killer set, too. But to dig at his ex-bandmates, Bobby sang "Rat Fink," which the Misfits used to cover. The Misfits responded by heckling Bobby from the side of the stage.

When the Misfits went on, Undead fans pelted them with ice cubes, beer cans, and bottles. Enraged, singer Glenn Danzig changed the lyrics to "Teenagers from Mars" on the spot, singing: *"Bobby Steele's an asshole fucking cunt! A fucking asshole cunt! Bobby Steele and the Undead suck!"*

Bobby and Lucy screamed at the Misfits from the Ritz's balcony. From the upstairs dressing room window, I got the crowd shouting, *"KISS! KISS! KISS!"* The Ritz bouncers went after Bobby, and a mini riot broke out in the balcony.

Doyle Wolfgang von Frankenstein, the Misfits's grotesquely buff guitarist, looked right up at me and gave me the finger. He shook his fist like he was going to beat me up.

"You better get outta here!" Carco yelled. "Go hide in the car."

I hightailed it out of the Ritz and locked myself in Javier's station wagon, which was parked a block away. Finally, the show was over, and Carco and Frawley came out with the gear.

"Good thing you took off," Carco said. "Those Misfits guys came upstairs looking for you."

I gulped. "Really?"

"Yeah, they were like, 'Where's the kid from Heart Attack? Where is he?'"

* * *

A few weeks later, I went to the Peppermint Lounge to see the U.K. Subs. Before the show, I hung out in the lobby, leaning against a wall near the door, looking out for friends.

Suddenly, to my horror, the Misfits marched into the lobby in leather jackets with the sleeves cut off to showcase their bulging muscles. They were fucking frightening. I shrank against the wall. But their bassist, Jerry Only, who was Doyle's brother, spotted me. He lumbered toward me. The other Misfits followed.

"You the kid from Heart Attack?" Jerry growled.

"I, uh, yeah," I managed to squeak out.

He put his gigantic fist up to my face and bellowed, "Great fuckin' show! Great fuckin' show!"

Chapter 15

Keep Your Hands Off of Me

I'm addicted to the hand jive
I've been living on the downstroke
—"Addicted"

As lenient as my mother was, she was from that generation that believed going to college was the answer to everything. I kept getting into trouble at school, and that upset her. All I cared about was going on tour again, but I knew she'd be devastated if I dropped out.

I was bitching to Andy Apathy about how much I hated my school while we were hanging out on Avenue A one night.

"You should go to Quintano's with me," Andy said. "It's a private school for musicians and actors, near Columbus Circle. It's pretty cheap, and they'll let you go on tour anytime you want."

Heart Attack now had write-ups in music magazines and newspapers. We'd been on the road and released a record. Technically, I qualified to attend the Leonard Quintano School for Young Professionals. Dr. Quintano founded the school in the early 1950s to cater to working teenage actors. It had a great reputation for a while, but by the 1980s it had degenerated into what Aerosmith singer Steven Tyler called "a school for fuck-ups like myself where you just had to show up to graduate."

It sounded perfect to me.

I talked Grandma Sara into paying the $1,500 tuition by

claiming that Quintano's was a prestigious music school—like Juilliard. I dropped the names of certain illustrious alumni someone her age might know: Sal Mineo, Patty Duke, Bernadette Peters. That sealed the deal.

Andy also told me that the Ramones got their signature picks from Manny's Music on 48th Street, so I started going there to buy picks and strings. Manny's was way bigger and cheaper than the music stores in Queens.

Forty-Eighth Street was Music Row, lined with stores displaying the most beautiful electric guitars in their big windows—real Fenders and Gibsons. I loved to walk down the sidewalk and stare at them, dreaming of the day I would finally own one.

There were peep shows just around the corner, luring me in with neon promises of *live nude girls* for only twenty-five cents. I was still a bit shy when it came to sex, but I was also a horny, curious fifteen-year-old. After buying strings at Manny's one afternoon, I ventured into my first peep show.

The setup was pretty simple: You buy tokens—four for a dollar—from the cashier, and walk down a dark circular hallway reeking of ammonia. It's lined with booths—each with its own door, small window, and meter box. When you drop a token into the meter, your window shade rises and you can see naked women dancing around in high heels. They press their bodies against the glass and get all provocative and sexy.

But before you know it, that shade comes down fast. You have to keep putting tokens in the meter if you want to take care of business.

This was wildly exciting for me, and I quickly got hooked. One afternoon, my mother took my sister and me to a Broadway play. Halfway through it I whispered, "Ma, I gotta go to the bathroom." I zipped over to the nearest peep show and did my thing.

Another time, that window shade came rolling down before I could finish—but I was out of money. I ran back to Manny's with four packs of guitar strings I had just bought. "I don't have fare for the train, can I please return one of these?" I begged the nice middle-aged lady behind the counter. She took pity on me and refunded me three dollars. I ran back to the peep show so I could get my nut and go home.

The only problem, besides my growing peep show habit, was the creepy men who lurked around the booths, trying to get a look at my teenage cock—or more. I didn't understand why they didn't just go to the gay peep right next door.

For protection, I started bringing Rizzo and Carco with me to Show World, a peep show palace on Eighth Avenue. The cleaning staff's T-shirts read: YOU DROP IT, WE MOP IT. Unfortunately, because the booths were in a circle, sometimes you'd catch your friend's face across the way pressed against the glass, staring bug-eyed at the girls. That wasn't exactly a turn-on.

I continued hitting the peep shows, but I also started meeting girls at Max's who actually liked me. I began seeing a nineteen-year-old named Caroline with large breasts and dyed black hair who was pretty fun and free. She lived in Staten Island. After our dates, we'd catch the Staten Island Ferry and make out on the windy ride across the water. Then we had to take a train to Caroline's neighborhood. We'd fool around on the grass outside her parents' house with our clothes on—or maybe off just a little.

This trip to Staten Island and back home to Queens took me around six hours—just to get a little action. A price I was happy to pay in those days.

I got mono, probably from passing around a beer at a gig or being run down from lack of sleep. I blamed Caroline, though, because the doctor told me mono was "the kissing disease." My mother put her foot down and made me stay home in bed. Heart Attack had to drop out of a big show at A7 with Reagan Youth, the Undead, and Kraut. Frawley was so mad that he got wasted at the show and passed out on the train.

After that, I decided to only get my loving out of magazines and peep shows. No more girls. Just focus on my band. Honestly, this decision brought me peace, because my sex drive felt like an anvil on my soul sometimes.

Javier and Dali got married, and Dali's sister Patty came up from Mexico City to spend the holidays with them. Even when she came on to me on New Year's Eve, I stuck to my guns.

By February, my militant celibacy had gone out the window. I started dating a cute, smart sixteen-year-old named Melanie who lived with her mother in Spanish Harlem. Melanie's dad wasn't around. She told me that he used to date Billie Holiday.

Melanie was half Black and half Jewish. When we met at the Mudd Club, I felt drawn to her warm brown eyes and soft olive skin. She had curly brown hair and wore combat boots with cardigan sweaters and tight blue jeans. She went to Bronx Science, like my father. She was pretty in a natural, no-makeup kind of way—but she wasn't ready to have sex.

I didn't really mind. I genuinely liked being with her—and we did mess around a lot in Javier's car, or in my bedroom when my mother wasn't home. We got pretty hot and heavy, without going all the way.

Tension was growing, though, between me and my mother. "You're always running somewhere. You always got one foot out the door!" she would yell.

Melanie's mother, on the other hand, invited me over

for dinner one night, and made steak with roasted Brussels sprouts and potatoes. I felt like the king of the world, being waited on by my girlfriend's mom in the big city. After dinner, I used their kitchen phone to call home and ask my mother if I had any messages. She said Danny wanted me to call him at some number I didn't recognize. We had plans to maybe meet up later, so I dialed it right away.

"Chelsea Hotel," some man grunted. He put me through to a room and Danny answered.

"Jesse," he whispered, "Remember Roxy? From Max's?" Sexy older women at the clubs loved to hit on us teenage boys—and Danny loved them back. They really went for his cute smile and strawberry-blond curls.

"Yeah, Roxy, right," I whispered into the phone, turning toward the wall. I had a feeling I wasn't going to want Melanie or her mother to hear this conversation.

"Man, she's got a shaved pussy!" Danny told me. "And this other chick is going at it with a vibrator!"

Here I was, thinking I was a big man, eating Brussels sprouts uptown. "I can't talk right now," I whispered. "I'm at Melanie's."

"Oh . . . Oh my God . . . fuuuuck!" Danny groaned. He dropped the phone.

I hung up, thinking: *That bastard. He's totally outdoing me.* When I turned around, Melanie and her mother were staring at me. I quickly wiped the disappointed look off my face and gave them what I hoped was a sweet, wholesome smile. "Great dinner, Mrs. Hart," I said. "Can I help you clean up?"

I ran into Earl, the Bad Brains drummer, at A7 a few nights later and gave him a copy of Heart Attack's new record.

"God is dead, huh?" Earl said, shaking his head.

Oh shit, I thought, remembering Earl's brother H.R. and his Bible.

But Earl thanked me and took my record anyway. He and H.R. were always supportive like that.

The Bad Brains had a big show coming up at Irving Plaza. It was their first time headlining such a large venue. I was surprised—and really honored—when they asked Heart Attack to open.

Before the show, Poss met up with H.R., who was at 171-A putting the finishing touches on an effigy of Ronald Reagan. Poss and H.R. marched this thing across town to Irving Plaza and hid it onstage. They tied a rope noose around its neck, and Poss climbed up a ladder backstage and threw the rope over the lighting rig.

At this point, the Bad Brains were heavily into Rastafari. The dressing rooms upstairs were crowded with Rastas sporting dreadlocks, and the air was thick with spliff smoke. The Bad Brains had adopted the vegetarian "ital is vital" diet and their catering tables were loaded with fruits and vegetables. There was no alcohol, which the Rastas called "hellfire water."

Everyone in our scene loved the Bad Brains. We were thrilled to see them take this giant step up. Irving Plaza was packed. I felt ready for that big stage after playing the Ritz—except that I had stupidly blown my voice out the night before, screaming at a show.

Even though I sounded raspy, our set was a blast. Boots flew past my face as kids dove off the stage nonstop. Melanie and Dali beamed at us from the sidelines. Scanning the crowd, I noticed lots of people I'd never seen before. This thing was really growing.

After our set, I grabbed Melanie and ran back downstairs just in time for the Bad Brains. The sidelines and even the stage were jammed with fans. The Bad Brains preached unity in their songs, and they meant it. Before they came around, you wouldn't dream of climbing up onto the stage.

But the Bad Brains welcomed their fans onstage. They were the first band I'd ever seen break down that barrier so completely. That night, we all felt so connected. I loved watching the place explode while they tore it up.

At the end of their show, H.R. grabbed that rope and sent old Reagan spiraling up to the ceiling—and the crowd went wild.

Chapter 16

Tao of Love and Sex

Waiting on a midnight bus
Running from the chickenhawks
—"Whitestone City Limits"

Every Wednesday morning, I got up early and hung around the corner deli until stacks of the *Village Voice* were dropped off the back of a truck. I couldn't wait to scour the club section to find out what cool bands were playing. That's how I found out that one of my favorite British bands, the Angelic Upstarts, were playing with Black Flag at the Left Bank in Mount Vernon. The show was on Sunday—but Monday was Memorial Day, so I figured my mother wouldn't get too bent out of shape.

Danny, Anthony, and I hopped in Hal Janney's car for the half-hour drive north. Hal was a generous guy whose family owned a German deli in Queens. We called him Hal the Show because he had taken over Tim Sommers's radio program.

The Left Bank was literally an old bank, converted into a roomy venue with a big sound system. The Angelic Upstarts were about to go on when Danny and I both spotted a pretty girl with shoulder-length blond hair standing by the stage. She had an upturned nose, wide cheekbones, and green eyes ringed with black eyeliner. She wore plaid pants, black boots, and a ripped white T-shirt with MOBILE OIL INVITES YOU TO BECOME AN ANARCHIST scrawled on it in black marker. Even in her punk clothes, there was something classically beautiful about her. She reminded me of iconic blondes like Marilyn Monroe and Debbie Harry, who seemed completely unobtainable.

"Wow," I said quietly.

"I'm gonna go talk to her," Danny announced.

Fuck, I thought. Just watching him walk over to her made me crazy. As soon as Danny left her side to go shout at some friends, I sauntered over, trying to look cool and casual, and introduced myself.

Her name was Lisa, she told me in a soft, whispery voice. Before she could say anything else, I blurted, "I have a band called Heart Attack."

"Oh, I've heard of you guys," she said.

The Angelic Upstarts came on—and I was so excited to watch them with this cool girl. Unfortunately, they played with zero energy while the singer ragged on the audience and bitched about the USA.

"These guys suck!" I yelled to Lisa. "You wanna go outside?" She nodded.

It was a warm, sultry night. I walked Lisa through the parking lot, and around to the side of the building. She stood against the limestone wall and looked up at me. I leaned in and kissed her. A light misty rain began to fall as we stood there making out, lost in the moment. Summer was coming, you could smell it in the rain.

I felt an intense thrill kissing Lisa. She was so different from anyone I had ever been with before. As I reached down and caressed her legs, I felt this powerful surge of excitement. It was magnetic, and like a dream.

I was ignoring my friends, but I didn't care. I kept kissing Lisa until it started raining harder. We laughed, holding on to each other, and ran back into the club.

* * *

Lisa and I were inseparable that summer of 1982. I wanted to be with her all the time. I loved the way she smelled, spoke, moved—everything about her. She was Irish–Puerto Rican, and lived in a tight one-bedroom in Inwood with her mother and older sister, near the last stop on the A train. Her mother slept on the couch, like mine had for years.

When Lisa and I weren't together, we talked on the phone for hours. That drove both our families nuts. I stopped calling Melanie altogether. Lisa didn't understand why a certain cute girl in combat boots shot her dirty looks when we were out at shows.

Lisa was shy and quiet at first, but I learned pretty fast that she had a great mind, and a wide-ranging love of books, music, and art. That made me even crazier about her. She turned me on to albums I'd never really listened to before, like Bob Dylan's *Blood on the Tracks* and Patti Smith's *Horses*.

Lisa worked at FLIP, a new-wave clothing store next to the 8th Street Playhouse. I'd pick her up at the end of her shifts and we'd find a quiet stoop and hang out—holding hands, talking, and kissing into the night—until one of us had to go home.

One evening, Lisa and I rode with Hal to see the Dead Kennedys at the Paramount in Staten Island. As the show was letting out, a bunch of teenagers with baseball bats charged out of the pizza place across the street. They ran through the theater's parking lot smashing car windows and beating the shit out of any punk they could grab. Hardcore kids took the chains off their boots and fought back. The whole parking lot was a bloody brawl.

Lisa and I ran and jumped into Hal's car. He swerved around the fighting, and we tore out of there. That was another thing I loved about Lisa: She wasn't just a sexy girl. She was someone I could run down the street with, a partner in crime. Still, I always made sure she got home safe. After midnight, the A train made all local stops through Harlem and Washington Heights. Guardian Angels patrolled the trains in their red berets and baseball jackets, but they never made me feel any safer. And the transit cops could be real assholes. They were on the bottom of the police totem pole, and resented it.

When Lisa and I finally reached 207th Street, I'd walk her up what the locals called Rape Hill. I'd get Lisa to her door and race back down, hoping to catch the train before it pulled out. It was always gone, and I'd have to wait forty-five minutes for the next one.

Lisa was a virgin when we met. We had hot, sweaty sex for the first time in my bedroom when no one was home, with the Bad Brains blasting from my boom box. I was determined not to lose it too fast. I kept it together by thinking, *I gotta be strong like H.R.*

After that, we had sex whenever and wherever we could.

"What's with those bites on your neck?" my mother demanded when I came out of the shower in a towel one afternoon. "What are those? Hicker bites?"

That's what she called hickeys.

"You got scratches on your back! Didja get in a fight with a cat or something?"

I zipped into my room before she could ask me any more uncomfortable questions.

I wanted to last longer in bed, so I watched Russ Meyer skin flicks, trying to figure out how a male actor could screw so long with a voluptuous woman riding him like crazy. It seemed impossible.

When I had sex with Lisa, I tried thinking about boring things I couldn't stand—like baseball. That didn't help, so I turned to one of the main sources of education in my life, the Clash. I read an interview with Joe Strummer in a magazine where he said he wrote the Clash song "Lover's Rock" after reading *The Tao of Love and Sex*. "It's a thin book," Joe said, "and a good one to get if you are a boy trying to become a man."

I raced over to East West Books on Fifth Avenue, bought a copy, and read it cover to cover. It recommended stuff like breathing slowly through your nose during sex, to "hold onto your chi." I tried these things with Lisa, and they kinda helped. I learned to slow down. If you start off too fast and wild, you'll probably blow it. But if you go slow and resist that initial urge, you can last much longer—maybe even go all night. Now I could focus on Lisa, and make sure she felt good, too.

I exploded onto the stage with so much pent-up energy that I blew my voice out right away sometimes. Now, if I was about to lose my voice, I dialed back my intensity with deep, slow breaths. It was a lot like sex. If I paced myself, I could sing all night.

Elton John was still one of my favorite singers, but I was embarrassed to tell Lisa—afraid she might think I was soft. But Elton was coming to Madison Square Garden, and I really wanted to take her.

So one day, when Lisa and I were sitting on a stoop, I worked up the nerve to say, "I gotta tell you, I really love Elton John."

"I do too," Lisa murmured, then giggled. "Is that uncool?"

At Madison Square Garden, Lisa and I held each other tight and cried through the whole show.

I started classes at Quintano's a couple weeks later. The

school had shrunk to five cubicles, fittingly located above *High Times* magazine on the eighth floor of 132 West 60th Street. The students were mostly bluffers pretending to be "young professionals"—except for a few working actors like Diane Lane. Poss got into Quintano's citing his "performances" with Reagan Youth. Basically, if you had the tuition, you were in.

I felt like such a big guy taking the subway to Columbus Circle. I liked looking at the skyscrapers, and joining the morning commuters walking briskly to their offices. And I really loved leaving my Queens tormentors in the dust.

Some of Quintano's teachers were very nice, like sweet old Mrs. Joyce. She came to see Heart Attack and Reagan Youth at Max's on a freezing Thanksgiving eve, and brought us hot soup. Her son was Ed Begley Jr., an actor everybody knew from the TV show *St. Elsewhere*. He stopped by her classroom sometimes and goofed around with us.

Quintano's still had these threadbare show biz connections, but the school was on its last legs. So was Dr. Quintano. He was in his nineties, wore thick Coke-bottle glasses, and doddered around shakily, using a cane. He was the kindest old man, but watching him navigate our tiny classrooms was like something out of *Young Frankenstein*.

Sometimes Poss and I would call in to Quintano's and say we were out on tour. Meanwhile, we were across the street in Central Park drinking forties with Jimmy Drescher, who went by Jimmy G. now. As long as we were "working," the teachers let us miss class and get homework instead. We never did any of the homework.

After school, I'd go home to take a quick nap and practice, before hopping the train back into the city for some show. My mother sensed something fishy, given that she never saw me crack a book.

"That Mickey Mouse bullshit school better be accredited for college!" she'd yell.

"I'm not going to college, Ma, I'm going on tour!" I'd yell back on my way out the door.

Lisa had been kicked out of Catholic school for standing up to some mean nuns. She was at McBurney now, a college-prep school just a few blocks from Quintano's. My classes ended at one p.m. I'd eat my lunch on the steps of the public library, between those two big stone lions that watch over Fifth Avenue. Then I'd wander around the neighborhood until I could pick Lisa up at three.

On chilly fall days, we walked around holding each other, or took the subway to her mother's apartment in Inwood. Lisa's mom was into yoga, and had healthy stuff in the fridge I'd never seen before—like yogurts and avocados. I usually split before she got home from work; she probably wondered who was eating all her food.

As winter set in, it got too cold to hang out on the streets. I really wanted to find someplace where we could spend the night together. I managed to save up thirty-two dollars from my gas station job to get a room at the run-down Hotel Earle on Washington Square.

Lisa told her mother that she was sleeping over at a friend's that Saturday. It felt great to spend the whole night with Lisa in our own room. The next morning, we went for omelets and French fries at the Waverly Diner. Then we sat by the fountain in windswept Father Demo Square on Carmine and Bleecker, bundled in our winter coats, imagining what it would be like to live downtown.

It was great to have friends at school like Andy and Poss. But Andy wanted to be Dee Dee Ramone so bad. Andy dressed just like him in a motorcycle jacket over cropped tank tops, tight blue jeans, and white sneakers. Rumor had it Dee Dee used to turn tricks on the loop in Midtown for drug money.

One afternoon, I was staring out the window during class and I saw two town cars pull up. They idled alongside our building until some boys from Quintano's came down and quickly got into the cars.

Sometimes I'd be sitting in class and men in suits would enter and silently point to certain male students. Those boys would get up and follow them out the door. The teachers ignored these interruptions.

Andy clued me in one day while we were hanging out in the hall after biology class: "Hey Jesse, you wanna get rid of that SG copy and buy a Gibson, right?"

"Yeah!" I said.

"You know how those men come into class sometimes and pick out a few guys?"

"Yeah . . . ?"

"Man, they take you down to Atlantic City in those fancy black cars. You wanna get some money? Come with us."

I stared at Andy.

"These bored rich ladies will pay to suck on your balls for hours while their husbands are playing blackjack," he explained.

I was at a rare loss for words.

"And once in a while you gotta be with a man."

"I think I'll stay in biology," I said.

Chapter 17

Citizen of the World

*I'm up on 24th Street
And I'm looking at a life
—"Meet Me at the End of the World"*

False Prophets singer Stephan Ielpi had six-inch black fingernails on his right hand. He patched them with superglue when they cracked, then added another lumpy coat of black nail polish. He wore a military officer's cap and knee-high motorcycle boots. His nose was pierced with an A-for-anarchy stud, and he sported a sandy-blond Charlie Chaplin—or dare I say Hitler?—mustache with long scraggly ends. Stephan carried a walking stick topped with a cracked monkey skull named Szandor—also held together with superglue.

He told me he developed his bizarre look to scare off the Jamaican toughs who used to beat him up when he was growing up in Flatbush. "If they think you're crazy, they'll leave you alone," he said.

Stephan got kicked out of Catholic school for sawing a desk in half. He was the most theatrical performer in the punk scene. He also had a heart of gold and was funny as fuck. Behind Stephan's eccentric exterior was a sweet guy who cared a lot. He kept an eye on the girls and smaller kids in the pit, shoving away some of the rougher guys to make sure they didn't get steamrolled.

When bands like Agnostic Front or Warzone played

CBGB, the crowd in front of the stage got pretty crazy. Agnostic Front's singer was a real pit-starter; he got everybody moving in a circle. Bassist Diego would rip off his bass and leap offstage into the fray, thrashing wildly. The kids in the pits were just as wild. Russian Jimmy Contra, skinny as a rail but strong as a bull, had this fast, aggressive skank—you didn't want to get in his way. Little Eric Casanova wrote *CRO-MAGS* on his forehead in black Sharpie and did the creepy crawl, wrecking anybody who stepped in his path. Willie No Edge danced like a chicken in his sleeveless leather jacket with a vacant shock-treatment stare and a cigarette dangling from his mouth. Some guys took cheap shots at Willie in the pit, but he always stood his ground. Tiny Claudette in her crew cut and combat boots moshed it up with all the guys. Nick Marden stood off to the side, headbanging with one arm wrapped around his torso, swinging his other fist up and down.

Once, at three in the morning, Willie No Edge walked up to me with his Frankenstein stare. "I got laid last night," he droned, and pointed at his ragged leather jacket. "Ya wanna smell my lapel?"

Another night at CBGB, Stephan waved Szandor in my direction, motioning me over. "Giorgio, this is Jesse Malin, the singer for Heart Attack. He needs a rehearsal space."

Giorgio Gomelsky looked up at me from his chair and smiled warmly. He was a husky man in his late forties with twinkling brown eyes and a neat black mustache and goatee. "Wonderful to meet you, Jesse, wonderful!" he said in a booming Russian accent. "You must come to the house."

Later, Stephan bent my ear about how Giorgio had managed the Yardbirds and the Rolling Stones in London, and produced obscure art-rock bands like Gong and Magma. This sounded like bullshit to me. But an affordable rehearsal space in the city was a near-impossible find, so when Giorgio invited me and Lisa over for a Bastille Day party, we went. Neither of us knew what the hell Bastille Day was.

In time, I learned that everything Stephan had told me about Giorgio was true. He had used a hefty royalty payment from the Yardbirds to buy a small industrial building on West 24th Street in Chelsea. Giorgio lived upstairs, and rented out the downstairs space to bands, and an S&M club called Paddles.

Lisa and I didn't know any of this as we climbed the dark narrow stairs to Giorgio's loft. I was sweating in the July heat in my leather jacket, black jeans, and boots. Lisa was wearing a plaid schoolgirl skirt with combat boots and her favorite Patti Smith T-shirt.

"Welcome, Jesse, welcome!" Giorgio shouted as we entered his lair. He was at the stove with a cigarette dangling from his lips, stirring the largest pot of soup I'd ever seen. There were open bottles of red wine on a round coffee table, and some skinny guy in a dinner jacket was stretched out on a leather couch. An enormous hound rubbed up against Lisa's legs, knocking her onto a beat-up love seat.

"Urzo, don't be a beggar for love!" Giorgio hollered dramatically, as the dog tried to climb into Lisa's lap.

I heard footsteps on the stairs, and Giorgio called out, "Ricardo Inferno!" In walked singer Richard Hell.

Wow, I thought, *that's cool*. I took a second look at the guy on the couch. He was New York Dolls singer David Johansen. *Wow*, I thought, *that's really cool*. I smiled at him.

Johansen sneered at me and rolled his eyes, with a look that seemed to say, *What are these kids doing here?*

Giorgio came over and sat down holding a glass of wine. He and Johansen launched into a pretty funny bit, with Giorgio pretending to be Johansen's shrink. Johansen played along in a gravelly rasp, sounding like that lounge-singer character Buster Poindexter he came out with a few years later.

Giorgio turned his attention to me. "There's something about you, Jesse. I think you're going to do a lot of things."

I can't overstate the importance of hearing something so encouraging from a grown-up when you're used to people putting you down. What Lisa and I came to love most about Giorgio was that even though we were only fifteen, he treated us like adults and invited us into his world.

Javier called him "the Russian," as in, "When we gonna visit the Russian?"

Every time we dropped by, Giorgio had another crazy idea percolating.

"Jesse! We're going to redo *West Side Story*, with graffiti artists and rappers as the Jets and hardcore punks as the Sharks. I'm going to bring Joseph Papp from the Public Theater here and put him on a big chair—way up high. He's going to love it!"

Giorgio wanted me and Stephan to help him write this *West Side Story* revival, and star in it. Unfortunately, I nixed the idea as somehow racist, pushing lame stereotypes of both rappers and punks. I was too uptight back then to get it. It probably would have been great.

Giorgio was a radical madman, our crazy uncle, his eyes constantly lighting up with wild ideas. His passionate belief in me and my friends as artists gave us confidence. I always left his company feeling inspired, even if I rolled my eyes at his outlandish plans and rarely took his advice. When you're young, you always think you know better.

I also learned that Giorgio wasn't actually Russian. He had been born on a ship while his parents were fleeing Soviet Georgia. His father, a Ukrainian doctor, had been blacklisted as an antifascist. Giorgio's mother was a French hat designer.

As refugees, the Gomelskys had lived in Syria, Egypt, and Italy before settling in Switzerland. Giorgio truly was a citizen of the world.

Stephan and I heard that some big-shot promoter was charging fifteen dollars per ticket for an all-ages hardcore New Year's Eve bash at Irving Plaza, headlined by Canadian band D.O.A. We were disgusted by this outrageous cover charge, and the attempt to co-opt a night that was special to our scene.

We decided to throw an "Opposition Party" at Giorgio's and charge five bucks to get in. Giorgio was delighted with this idea, and gave us his blessing. A more sensible adult might have balked at inviting hundreds of punks to party at his house on New Year's Eve. But Giorgio loved the underground and the underdog. If you were about art, not money, he opened his home and his heart to you.

Reagan Youth, the Misguided, and False Prophets were going to play. "What about Heart Attack?" Stephan asked.

At first, I didn't want Heart Attack to play because we weren't ready yet to unveil our new lineup. Danny had just joined on guitar. His friend Paul Pittman—who called himself "Pablo Depraved"—was replacing John Frawley on bass. But I did have a new song called "English Cunts." It was my kiss-off to British punks who claimed the Sex Pistols invented punk rock—when everybody knows it was the Ramones. Javier championed the Pistols like some blue blood, just because he used to live in London. That drove me nuts.

"Put us down as the English Cunts," I told Stephan.

Frawley had quit after getting into a fight with Javier while we were making a new record. Not only did he quit—he snuck into the studio early the next morning and stole the tape. Then he joined the military and shipped out.

I didn't hear from Frawley for decades. In 2022, though, he came to New York and met me and Javier for dinner. Frawley walked in carrying a ziplock bag and laid it on the table. Inside was a reel of tape in pristine condition. "I'm sorry about this, guys," he said. "I've carried this with me all over the world, and I've always kept it safe."

I gave him a big hug, and the three of us had a great time reminiscing.

Stephan made one of his wacky collage fliers for the Opposition Party. After printing a stack at the copy shop on Broadway, we mixed fifty-cent packets of wheat paste with water in an empty paint bucket and hit the streets. We slapped fliers up all over downtown with an old paintbrush—keeping our eyeballs peeled for the cops. If we ran low on paste—and no pizza place or bar would let us in to get water—we'd piss in the bucket to mix another batch and keep going.

Bands fought relentless wheat-paste wars on the streets. You'd put up fliers, then circle around fast to make sure some rival band hadn't pasted over them. If they had, you'd go back and slap your fliers up over theirs—and hope another band coming up the block didn't cover them up again.

Back at Giorgio's, we built a stage out of plywood nailed to four old speaker cabinets, and hung lights covered with colored gels from the hardware store. We dragged all our gear onto the stage for the bands to share. Our girlfriends brought in cases of the cheapest beer they could find.

On New Year's Eve, our party was already mobbed by nine p.m. When the police arrived while I was working the door, I thought for sure the jig was up. False Prophets guitarist Peter Campbell, who was thirty and looked like a teacher, ran over to help me out. He spoke with the officers very politely, while discreetly shoveling cash into their hands from the cigar box stuffed with money we had collected. The cops quickly went on their way.

Wow, I thought, *that's really how it goes down*. I picked up tips that night about how to throw a party that would serve me well for years to come.

"This is your lab-or-a-tory, Jesse," Giorgio would say. "Use it to conduct experiments."

Once the bands hit our makeshift stage, the crowd became a sea of slam-dancing, beer-sloshing maniacs. Some idiots set off M-80s in the upstairs bathroom, blowing up one of Giorgio's toilets.

During the Misguided's set, a drunk man wearing a fedora wandered in off the street and got caught up in the crowd. Some kids grabbed his hat and tossed it back and forth, while he lurched around in vain trying to grab it. The fedora wound up hanging off the headstock of Carco's bass. Enraged, this guy climbed onstage, pulled out a big knife, and lunged at Carco. Carco dodged him without missing a beat, and the man fell to the floor.

Stephan hopped onstage and grabbed a mic. The Misguided stopped playing. "This guy tried to stab Carco!" Stephan shouted, pointing one black six-inch fingernail accusingly at him. The Misguided roared back into their song.

The man looked up at Stephan and completely freaked out. He bolted upright and ran off, shoving his way through the crowd in a panic. He didn't make it too far before some kids caught him, stomped on him pretty hard, and threw him out.

After midnight, even more people poured into our party—including D.O.A.'s singer and guitar player. They were both really tall, and made quite the entrance in their shiny cardboard New Year's Eve top hats. They had left their own party for where the real fun was.

When the Misguided left the stage, Jimmy G.—always the wildest dancer in the pit—grabbed the mic and yelled, "*Wild thing! You make my dick sting!*" while Harley from the Stimulators bashed the drums, Adam Mucci got on bass, and "Uncle Al" Morris played guitar.

We were witnessing the birth of a great new band: Murphy's Law. Those guys made up their famous song "Fun" right there on the spot. That's the great thing about punk rock: a kid in the crowd can jump onstage and create a band that winds up touring the world for forty years.

The entire fabulous mess of a night was unforgettable. We made enough money to pay every band that played, and give some to Giorgio, too. Jimmy, Lisa, and I staggered out into the dawn around six a.m. I was promptly hit in the head with a flying beer bottle, but I was too happy for it to bother me.

Chapter 18

Young Anarchists (in Love)

The politics of punk rock church
We were so idealistic
But somehow only saw the worst
—"Almost Grown"

To this day, I still can't hear the line "*Most of all you've got to hide it from the kids*" from the Simon & Garfunkel song "Mrs. Robinson" without choking up.

When my mother got sick, she didn't tell me or my sister for a long time. I gleaned the truth from eavesdropping on her kitchen phone calls. I heard the fear in her voice.

After Grandma Renee died young, my mother was afraid that she would get cancer, too. When she was diagnosed with breast cancer at thirty-seven, she hid it from us kids, especially Juliet, who was scared of her own shadow. Scared of monsters under the bed, scared to go to school, scared of everything—that was sweet, gentle Juliet.

Eventually, my mother couldn't hide her illness from us anymore. She had a single mastectomy, followed by chemotherapy. She had a hard time with losing her hair and the surgical devastation of her body. Mastectomies were crude back then. She looked like she'd been attacked with a chainsaw. She had a long, jagged scar across her torso, and no reconstruction—just a prosthetic breast to wear inside her bra.

I remember looking at Lisa and thinking, *If something this awful happened to her, would I still love her just as much?* I knew the answer: nothing could change how I felt about her.

We were madly in love, constantly looking for places to fool around. That must have been hard on my mother while she was going through this. She wasn't always so nice to Lisa.

I think my mother felt robbed of her beauty, and perhaps any chance to find a real partner. Frank Shira still came around, when he could. He never abandoned her—but he never left his wife, either.

When my mother went into remission, we were overjoyed. But my sister was still scared, and would beg, "Mommy, please, promise me that you're not gonna die."

"I promise you I'm not gonna die," my mother said every time.

On an icy January day, Paul, Danny, Javier, and I lugged our gear from Javier's beat-up blue station wagon into Radio City Music Hall's side entrance on 50th Street. I had just turned sixteen, and Heart Attack was about to make a new record.

Ed Bahlman produced arty bands like the Bush Tetras and Liquid Liquid. After seeing Heart Attack play the Ritz, Ed booked us into Plaza Sound on Radio City's eighth floor. I couldn't believe we'd made it all the way from crooked Northern Boulevard to shiny Rockefeller Center.

As I dragged my little amp into the studio, I was floored by its massive size. The walls were covered with mirrors and ballet barres for Rockettes rehearsals. I was more excited that the Ramones had made their first album here. Ace Frehley from KISS recorded "Back in the New York Groove" here, too.

Danny and I took off like a couple of chimps, running down the stairs and dashing all over the Radio City stage. I climbed a narrow iron ladder until I reached a catwalk high above the stage. I charged across it with total disregard for life and limb. We finally calmed down enough to return to the studio. Javier eyed us with disdain, shaking his head as he tuned his drums.

With Ed at the helm, wearing some funky outfit that looked like his pajamas, we tracked six songs. Javier's ferocious drumming on "From What I See" is one of the first blast beats ever recorded. Danny added tight, tough-fisted guitar. *Keep Your Distance* was Heart Attack's most political record yet.

Anarchy was in the air. The circle-A was spray-painted on walls all over downtown. It decorated T-shirts and jackets at trendy stores. But Lisa and I were interested in real anarchists, not the poseurs shopping for anarchy at the mall I mocked in my song "Trendies."

We loved the film *Anarchism in America*, which taught us that the US was founded on anarchist principles of freedom and independence. Giorgio hipped us to the French Situationists and *The Society of the Spectacle* by Guy Debord. These influences were antiauthoritarian—but also intellectual. They opened my mind to an entire world of subversive ideas and actions beyond punk rock.

Lisa and I ran with a group of earnest kids who passionately believed that we could change the world. We believed in a free, self-governing society based on trust, not rules. We hung out in bookstores and on stoops dissecting these ideas. We hated the right-wing politicians who were thirsty for war.

In just two years, I would be required to register with the military. As a child, I had seen soldiers' bodies come home in boxes from the Vietnam War on TV. Now, I was scared that I could be drafted into Reagan's dirty wars in Central America.

Lisa and I attended every antiwar and human rights demonstration in town, and all the Rock Against Racism and Rock Against Reagan shows. Heart Attack played at some of them, too.

My mother got fed up with my nonstop preaching. "I don't wanna hear that garbage in my house! What, are you being brainwashed by communists? Go down to Washington Square and stand on a soapbox if you wanna talk that crap."

Some anarchists railed against eating meat, but I conveniently ignored that. I lived on McDonald's and White Castle burgers. My heroes, the Bad Brains, were vegetarian, but I associated that with their Rastafari beliefs.

One day, though, I noticed a bumper sticker on Nick Marden's stove: *LOVE ANIMALS, DON'T EAT THEM*. It stopped me in my tracks—and made me think. I had never connected a hamburger to a living being before. I bought a copy of *What's Wrong with Eating Meat?* at St. Mark's Bookshop. After reading it, I couldn't kill a cow to get a burger anymore. I switched my diet to bagels, falafel, and deep-fried tofu burgers. I had yet to learn Vegetarianism 101: eat some vegetables.

Lisa went vegetarian six months before I did. She was into feminism, too, and fighting the patriarchy. Our pal Philo Virgin pressured me to sell my "sexist" rock albums. Philo wore the same utilitarian outfit every day: black wool cap over shaved head, plain black T-shirt, black pants, black boots. No badges or chains. "You gotta get rid of all this Zeppelin and Aerosmith," he declared, rifling through the albums in my bedroom. "These records are degrading to women! . . . The Dead Boys gotta go, too."

"Why?" I cried. "They're punk rock!"

"'Caught with the Meat in Your Mouth?' That's punk?" Philo sneered. "And fuck Iggy Pop—screwing teenage groupies. These pigs treat women like objects."

"Not Iggy!" I groaned, as Philo tossed *Raw Power* onto the reject pile.

This was just the beginning of us young anarchists becoming judgmental jerks.

Lisa and I started an anarchist collective with Philo, Stephan from False Prophets, my bass player Paul Pittman, and Sharon Gannon—an artist and animal-rights activist who waitressed at Life Cafe. We held meetings at Stephan's grimy ground-floor apartment on Avenue B.

Stephan's bedroom was a horny hoarder's paradise, filled with stacks of dirty magazines. Lisa and I decided this was unacceptable for an anarchist. We hatched a direct-action plan—for the cause. We would meet at Columbus Circle at precisely three o'clock on Friday and head downtown.

We exited the subway at Astor Place, marched over to Stephan's apartment, and banged on the door. He opened it in his pajamas, rubbing his eyes.

"Hey," Stephan yawned, "what's up?"

"We need to talk, man," I said.

Stephan sighed. "All right. Come on in."

Lisa and I sat down while Stephan poured himself a mug of coffee and went to get dressed. When he came out, Lisa announced, "You need to throw out all your porn."

"I . . . what?" Stephan muttered, taken aback. He shot me a pleading look.

"Yeah, man," I said. "You gotta get rid of it. If you wanna be a real anarchist."

Being anarchists, we had to debate this for a good hour. Eventually, Stephan caved. Lisa and I supervised as he reluctantly stuffed his magazines into half a dozen Hefty trash bags. He trudged unhappily out the door with each bag, and tossed it into the dumpster down the street.

Mission accomplished, Lisa and I headed to St. Marks to sell my "sexist" records on the sidewalk. People sold used clothes, books, and records dirt cheap on sheets and blankets from Broadway to Second Avenue. Some of the stuff was definitely hot.

Once, someone broke into Javier's van and grabbed my motorcycle jacket—the first one I ever had made of real leather. That jacket meant the world to me. I had painted *MASSACRE*—one of my song titles—on the back in big white letters. The next day, Javier and I spotted a guy strutting along St. Marks wearing my jacket. We chased him down and he grudgingly handed it over. He had bought it for twenty bucks off some sidewalk-selling junkie.

Lisa and I hung out on the sidewalk all day sometimes—selling our stuff, drinking beer, and joking around with characters like Jerry the Peddler, Geneva Unconventional, and Matt Zombie. I liked selling things I didn't want anymore, as a stepping stone into my life's next chapter. It felt freeing to let things go. Another fun way to make a little money just hanging out.

The sidewalk wasn't some cozy suburban garage sale, though. There were lots of crazies wandering around. And if you set up in front of a shop, look out. The owner might charge out and kick your things into the street screaming, "You're blocking my store, assholes! Get the fuck outta here!"

Paul Pittman was a smart kid from Great Neck whose family had a little money. Paul got into New York University and moved into Weinstein Hall on University Place. I informed him that since we were all anarchists, Lisa and I were moving in, too. Share the wealth and all that.

We dragged Paul's mattress onto the floor for me and Lisa. Paul slept on the box spring. Philo crashed in Paul's dorm room, too, sometimes. Paul's roommate, Adam Dubin, wasn't thrilled about this anarchist incursion, but he tolerated us.

Adam's friend Rick Rubin lived down the hall. Rick blasted heavy rock 24-7 through giant PA speakers in his closet-sized room while he skipped classes and built a studio in there. I knew Rick from his band the Pricks. He used to call my house asking to play with Heart Attack.

"Ma," I'd yell when I got home from school, "did anybody call?"

"Yeah, Rick the prick."

"Really, Ma? Come on."

"Yeah, really. Rick the prick."

"Stop, Ma!"

I thought she was pulling my leg, because she was always teasing me that Jello Biafra had called. She loved saying his ridiculous name. The joke was on her the day Jello actually called our apartment.

Rick started recording his new band Hose—slow and sludgy, with lots of screechy feedback—in his room at ear-splitting volume. He hardly ever left the dorm, except to get food or check out rappers at the Roxy on 18th Street. Paul and I bombed his room with toilet paper a couple times when he did.

Our little anarchist collective began meeting in the dorm lobby late at night, instead of at Stephan's place. Sometimes, when Rubin was walking through the lobby with his Cozy Burger bag, he'd stop to listen to us rant about veganism or some other "ism." Then he'd shake his head and take his cheeseburgers upstairs.

Rubin was friends with the front desk clerk, Mr. Ric, who kept track of the demos arriving for Rubin's new record label, Def Jam—like the cassette tape from a Queens teenager named LL Cool J.

Occasionally I'd grab a tray at the cafeteria and pretend I was a student. I also snuck into a film class at Tisch Hall called "Scorsese/Coppola." The professor would talk about *Apocalypse Now* or *The Godfather* for a half hour, show the film, and discuss it afterward. I thought this was the greatest thing ever. Somehow, I never got caught.

A stocky woman in her twenties with a stubbly mohawk and a nose ring joined our anarchist collective. Her name was Laura A—for Anarchy, naturally. Like all of us, Laura had some damage and rage fueling her passion for protest. I had the feeling she'd been badly abused growing up.

I crashed at Laura's place once after a show. She climbed on top of me during the night wearing a sheer tutu with no panties, and started grinding away. I was freaked out, and played dead while Laura did her humping turtle dance. She finally gave up and went away.

Our collective preached against "physicalism." That's what we called judging people by their appearance. We argued that you should be attracted to someone's great politics, even if you find them physically unappealing. All I can say is, it didn't work for me.

We meant well. But we became obsessed with political correctness, and outdoing each other. *Don't shop at that store. Don't eat at that restaurant. Can't wear leather. Can't listen to any band on a major label.* So many rules.

Eventually, I realized that if the Clash hadn't been on a major label, the world would have never heard *Sandinista!* Artists like John Lennon and Bob Dylan weren't sellouts. They used the system to fuck the system—and got their message out to millions.

Being anarchists also meant Lisa and I shouldn't "own" each other—or feel jealous. We started sleeping with other people, including each other's best friends. We pretended everything was fine, but inside we were two kids aching, heartbreaking, and wrecking ourselves. We tried to be perfect, and forgot that we were human. Friends like Lyle and Danny started laughing at us and edging away, calling Lisa my Yoko.

You preach what you need to learn. In the end, our judgmental bullshit controlled us as much as any government ever could.

In spite of all this drama, we organized the first-ever Anarchy Festival to ring in 1984. We rented the New York Theatre Ensemble on East 4th Street. We booked bands, planned workshops, brought in vegan food, and arranged to show the film *Animal Farm*.

The A-Fest was a surprising success. People flew in from around the world, and it was packed day and night. Laura A was in charge of collecting the money. We covered all our expenses, and then some.

But the next day, Laura A disappeared forever—and so did our cash. Like Stephan had written on the A-Fest flier: *ORWELL THAT ENDS WELL*

Chapter 19

The Angels of Van Dam Street

*Paulie's waiting to retire, smoking like a forest fire
Putting on the panties and the lipstick in his mother's room*
—"Mona Lisa"

My mother was thrilled when I actually graduated from Quintano's. She came with me to the graduation dinner at Luchow's in Midtown. We'd never been to such a fancy place with such horrible food. She still wanted me to go to college, but I was hell-bent on a life in music.

The hardcore scene was blowing up, but in the process it became really macho. Cement heads and suburban jocks who enjoyed beating people up dominated the mosh pits, wrecking the unity that had made our scene so special. Gangs from all over New York flooded into downtown to prey on the drunk jackasses running around everywhere. Things got so violent that the cops started closing 8th Street on weekends.

I wasn't sure what to do. I wanted to write songs that moved people—the way Elton John, Jim Croce, and the Clash had moved me. But I didn't know how to reconcile this with my political side. Then I heard Bruce Springsteen's *Nebraska*. I hadn't paid much attention to him, but that stripped-down album with just his voice and acoustic guitar really hit me. You could taste the starkness and hardness of American life in those songs. *Nebraska* was bleak, yet full of hope and romance, too.

My buddies ribbed me for liking "the Boss," especially

when *Born in the U.S.A.* came out. "Who is this Rambo motherfucker? You like this major-label bullshit?"

"Did you read the lyrics?" I'd retort. "He's writing about working-class people who are struggling. Half the songs are about people who wind up broken or in jail."

I dug into Billy Bragg and the Replacements—punks who weren't afraid to wear their hearts out on their sleeves. They gave me the courage to break up Heart Attack.

I bought a cheap acoustic guitar and started a new band called Hope with Ivan Martin and Jeffrey Z. The lineup eventually solidified into Carco on bass, Danny on guitar, and his brother, Michael Wildwood, on drums.

I basically moved into the cluttered rehearsal studio on Avenue B that Hope shared with False Prophets. It was a dusty former thrift store, with moldy carpeting and a janky roll-down gate. On cold nights, I used a lighter to melt the ice on the gate's padlock. I slept on a lawn chair and lived on expired yogurts and tofu I scrounged from my health-food-store job in Murray Hill, and vegan chili from Life Cafe on the corner.

Life Cafe was an oasis in the ghetto. The couple who ran it, David and Kathy, slept in the back—like Dave and Cathy from the Rat Cage. David had found a stack of old *LIFE* magazines in the basement. He shellacked the covers onto every inch of wall and on all the little wooden tables. The place was full of characters: poets, artists, punks, chess players, and junkies on the nod. Regulars like Billy Sleaze and Charlie Bananas sat there for hours, nursing cups of coffee while jazz played in the background. Billy was a leather boy, and Charlie went to jail for robbing a bodega down the street.

Rent, food, and dope were cheap in the East Village back then. It was a place where you could figure out who you were—or get really fucked up on drugs. Or both.

* * *

One night, Hope's rehearsal was interrupted by heavy pounding on our studio's flimsy plywood door. I cautiously cracked it open. A crew of Black teenagers in baggy pants and puffy sneakers came flooding in, right up in our faces. I was sure they were going to grab our guitars, pedals—everything we'd worked so hard to finally have.

"Yo, man," one kid shouted, "can we try your mics?"

I felt terrible for having assumed they were out to rob us. "Sure!" I said.

I set them up with three mics, and they were so excited to hear their voices loud and clear through our speakers. They started rapping and Michael put a beat behind them on the drums. We gave each other props and high fives, and the kids went on their merry way into the night.

Hope's first gig was at the Pyramid, a small, dark club on Avenue A where bands and drag queens like Lady Bunny and RuPaul performed. But when I approached the mic with my acoustic guitar, Jack Flanagan yelled, "Get that Mellencamp thing outta here!" Everybody laughed. My friends started calling me Jesse Cougar Malincamp.

I thought Hope sounded good, and we played some great shows, but I couldn't get any record labels interested. Nobody wanted to hear my sensitive songs—except maybe Lisa and my mom.

On Friday evenings, I busked in the First Avenue subway station for working stiffs headed home to Brooklyn, with my tattered guitar case open at my feet. I could make sixty or seventy bucks playing Elvis and Dion songs. I snuck in some Ramones, and a few Hope songs, too. The cops chased me away pretty often, though.

At night, I dug into the huge record collection False

Prophets bassist Steve Wishnia kept in the studio with his nice turntable. He was always so cool about letting me play his albums, as long as I put them back in alphabetical order. Wishnia had bushy hair and a matching soul patch. He wore round glasses that slid down his nose when he played bass.

"I'm losing tone . . . I'm losing tone," Wishnia would complain whenever the sound guy at some club made him turn down his giant bass amp.

One night, I came across a new Johnny Thunders record called *Hurt Me* in Wishnia's stack. I put it on the turntable. The album was haunting and achingly personal. Just Johnny and his acoustic guitar—like a punk-rock *Nebraska*. He still had his attitude and swagger, but he also sounded beautifully vulnerable—although at times he could sound like a whiny junkie trapped in a basement. Either way, something real here spoke to me.

Hurt Me was the kick I needed to trust my gut and go for it.

I met peace-punk siblings Vinny and Jeanette Vespole on St. Marks Place. They dressed head to toe in black, with badges pinned to their jackets and anarchist slogans scrawled on them.

Vinny was a big, affable bass player who wore his brown hair in tall liberty spikes stiff with soap. He was such a committed vegan anarchist that he wouldn't listen to any record without reading all the lyrics first to make sure the band was 100 percent politically correct.

Jeanette was a four-foot-eleven cutie with a powerful operatic voice. She and Vinny started the band A.P.P.L.E.—Anarchism, Peace, Pacifism, Liberty, Existentialism. Jeanette bleached her hair blond and changed her name to Jae Monroe.

Vinny and Jae invited Lisa and me to hang out at their parents' old brick row house on the ragged edge of Greenpoint, Brooklyn, near the garbage-truck depot. Nobody lived out there except working-class Poles and a few Italians.

I convinced my dad to lend me a thousand bucks to buy a rusty white Dodge van so I could start a moving business. Actually, I planned to use it to take Hope on tour. Now that I had wheels, Lisa and I went to the Vespole house on Van Dam Street a lot.

Vinny and Jae had an ex-military, cross-dressing brother named Paul. We called him Skel. He was thirty, and a security guard at Dow Jones & Co., across the street from the World Trade Center. Skel told us he was a lesbian trapped in a man's body. When he got high enough, Skel would strut out of his room dressed in drag, with the badass smirk of a woman who thinks she's a real head-turner.

Skel was a kind, generous soul. He took me and my sister out to dinner in the city many times. He bought all us kids tickets to shows we couldn't afford, like Robert Gordon at the Lone Star Cafe, and Roy Orbison at the Beacon Theatre. When I was short on money to make fliers, Skel printed them for me on a copier at the office when nobody was looking. After he got off work, I'd wait for him on the L train platform, at the last car on the line. When the train doors opened, Skel would toss me a big bag full of bundled fliers. I'd catch it and he would give me a wave through the window as the train pulled away.

Skel got his father a security-guard job at the *Journal*, too. Mr. Vespole was a short, tough Italian American who had done time for his part in robbing a fur truck. His job had been to hold a gun to the driver's head while his buddies ransacked the truck. Now, Mr. Vespole was a legit family man, married to Marge, a lovely Southern lady with a sweet

Tweety Bird voice. "I'm laying low now, Jesse," he'd joke with me. "Sometimes ya gotta lay low."

Mr. Vespole still had an ex-con's sense of humor. He loved to tell the story about the time he invited a coworker over for a home-cooked meal. As they drove through the dirty tunnel lined with unhoused people that led to Van Dam Street, Mr. Vespole's colleague—fearing he was about to get whacked—piped up nervously, "Tony, what godforsaken place are you taking me to?"

Mr. Vespole hated junkies because a junkie had ratted out his crew. But he didn't know his oldest son was one until he caught Skel stealing stuff to hock from Marge's jewelry box when he was short on cash for smack. Mr. Vespole held a gun to his son's head until Skel put every piece back in the box.

Mr. and Mrs. Vespole were always happy to see me, and that made me feel real good. They folded me into their crazy family—something I needed badly. They were my angels on Van Dam Street.

"In my day, people looked out for each other!" Mr. Vespole would shout. "People cared about each other. Now it's, *Hooray for me and fuck you. Hooray for me! And FUCK YOU!*"

He and Mrs. Vespole lived on the first floor. Vinny, Jae, and Skel lived upstairs, with a drum kit and PA system in their living room. I'd come over and Vinny would say, in his thick Brooklyn accent, "Let's make some shells and watch a bomb."

We'd cook up an aluminum pan of pasta shells with sauce, and go rent movies from the video store on Nassau Avenue. We watched *The Three Stooges*, Mel Brooks, and anything with Robert De Niro or Al Pacino. Then I'd get on the drum kit, Vinny would play bass, Jae sang, and we'd play every punk song we knew. Our thrash racket blasted down the row houses all the way to the BQE. I don't know how Mr. and Mrs. Vespole put up with it, but they were just happy to have their kids at home.

I liked to drink, but I had nothing on the Vespole boys. Skel tried hard to stay off smack, drinking booze instead. He would go into work bombed and pass out under his desk. Everyone covered for him because he was such a sweet guy.

Once, Mr. Vespole caught Skel passed out on the couch in full drag with a half-eaten can of tuna resting on his chest and a fork poking into his neck.

"I know ya need an outlet," Mr. Vespole screamed, "BUT THIS?"

When Vinny got drunk, he'd get what he called "the urge to destroy." We went to see Johnny Rotten's new band PiL play at L'Amour in Queens. Vinny climbed onstage, tackled Rotten, and knocked him on his ass for being a sellout. L'Amour's bouncers hauled Vinny off the stage and beat him bloody. Vinny just scrambled back onstage and knocked Johnny Rotten over again.

My friends and I all had a bit of "the urge to destroy." After a few drinks, we'd dive headfirst into steel trash cans or onto piles of garbage bags. One night, we pulled up to a bank in my van so I could use the ATM. On my way out, I kicked and smashed up the glass door and all the windows. We sped away laughing our heads off. I'd probably get caught on camera and go to prison for that today.

One sticky August night, Carco was out wheat-pasting for Hope when he ran into Vinny. Carco was sweat-soaked and cranky, and Vinny was drunk.

"That fuckin' place Mr. Beef!" Vinny roared. "Selling MEAT! I wanna wreck it!"

After a few pops from Vinny's fifth of whiskey, Carco

was down. They always looked pretty funny together: Carco skinny as a noodle and Vinny more like a well-stuffed ravioli.

They descended on Mr. Beef, a Second Avenue shop that sold Italian roast beef sandwiches. A big sign fifteen feet above the sidewalk displayed a cartoon Mr. Beef with his fork stuck in a giant sandwich stuffed with meat.

Carco polished off the whiskey and lobbed the bottle at Mr. Beef. It ripped right through him, trashing the sign. Vinny and Carco took off running, laughing the whole time. After that, Vinny called Carco "Mr. Beef"—or just "Beef" for short.

The Vespole kids ran wild, but Mr. Vespole knew how to track them down. He kept the numbers for all six pay phones outside the Gem Spa newsstand on St. Marks written down in the kitchen. When Mr. Vespole wanted to find his children, he called every pay phone until somebody picked up who knew where they were and promised to go tell them to get their asses home.

Chapter 20

Man with Van

*When your holidays are cold
And your family doesn't speak*
—"She's So Dangerous"

After my mother's cancer went into remission, my sister and I truly believed she was going to be fine. But her disease was like the monster in a horror movie: it kept coming back. To take care of her and Juliet, I moved back into our Whitestone apartment.

Juliet still lived in the small room off the kitchen, where she kept a collection of tiny figurines. It was her glass menagerie, and if you touched them, she would go crazy. My mother leaned on Juliet a lot, as if she were her teddy bear. I guess Juliet needed something of her own that no one else could touch.

I decided to use my van to make some money. I made a new flier:

*MAN WITH VAN
24-HOUR SERVICE
NO JOB TOO SMALL*

I put up fliers all over downtown, and at the Music Building on Eighth Avenue. I started picking up work carting bands to gigs.

The Music Building was Manhattan's biggest rehearsal

spot, with sixty-nine filthy studios inside. Metal, punk, and grunge blasted from those rooms onto Eighth Avenue and echoed off the concrete buildings like some industrial cacophony from hell.

The first time I helped a band load in, I came out and my van wouldn't start. I opened the hood. The battery was gone. I stood there in shock until a jittery crackhead bounced over to me.

"Hey, man, what's goin' on? You all right?" He peered over my shoulder at my engine. "Ah, looks like you need a battery, bro." He produced a battery, wrapped in a tattered garbage bag. "It's your lucky day, man! Got one right here. Five bucks."

I had no choice but to give the son of a bitch five bucks to get my battery back so I could drive home.

I started bringing Carco along to watch the van, so that I could help bands move their gear and watch their sets, which they really liked. My sideview mirrors were always getting broken off or stolen, so Carco would look out the window before I changed lanes in the city's insane traffic.

Carco liked hanging out all night, chain-smoking in the passenger seat. He was great company—full of fascinating stories about the city and rock-and-roll history. The bands all loved him. "It's a Carcopolis, you and me just live here," our friend Troy Lush used to say.

One of my regulars was an all-female polka-punk band called Das Fürlines that rehearsed at Giorgio's. The S&M club Paddles threw parties there on Saturday nights. We'd come from a gig and have to navigate through middle-aged characters in fetish gear getting tied up and—you guessed it—paddled.

I began booking moving jobs, too, with my buddy Pete Vivino. Pete had a shaved head and goatee, way before that was fashionable. He looked and sounded just like Egghead, the Vincent Price villain on the old *Batman* TV show. We were the most unlicensed of unlicensed movers. We moved friends in and out of Lower East Side squats. We did guerrilla midnight moves for people about to be evicted. We moved families out of eight-story tenements with no elevators. We carried sofa beds that popped open on narrow, airless stairways, and pianos and televisions that slid out of our sweaty hands. Dogs tried to bite us and we'd kick them away. We'd walk into an apartment and duck flying dishes as a couple was breaking up.

We once climbed six flights to find an old lady standing over a stinking piss-stained mattress we were too grossed out to touch. "It's only uuurine!" she shouted.

We moved clueless freshmen into NYU dorms in Greenwich Village who asked us where "the Village" was. We told our customers to be packed and ready to go, but often, when we arrived, the place was a wreck. We climbed countless stairs in sweltering heat from the Bronx to Newark, from Asbury Park to Staten Island. We never said no. We needed the money.

Summer turned to fall, and at least we weren't sweating our asses off so much. On a crisp autumn day, Pete and I got called to Barbra Streisand's swanky penthouse to move her bed into Manhattan Mini Storage. While I was taking in her spectacular view of Central Park, Pete snuck up behind me. I could smell the garlic from his mother's spaghetti sauce on his breath as he yelled in my ear, "Maaaalin, one song and this is all yours!"

Meanwhile, Danny and I managed to book Hope a one-week tour out to Ohio and back. We drove over to 23rd Street at the crack of dawn to pick up a U-Haul trailer for my van.

It was eerily quiet as Danny and I parked and walked west toward Tenth Avenue. Not a soul was on the street.

Suddenly, this nerdy guy with sandy-blond hair, wearing big glasses with clear frames, came walking straight toward us. It was Bernhard Goetz, the "subway vigilante" who had shot four Black teenagers in a subway car, claiming they'd tried to rob him. None of them died, but one boy was paralyzed. The jury found Goetz innocent of every charge, except for one count of carrying an unlicensed gun. Seeing him felt like a bad omen.

We were loading up the U-Haul at our rehearsal space when Bad Brains guitarist Dr. Know stepped out of the tiny Jamaican shop next door drinking a ginger beer. "Where you guys headed?"

"On tour!" I yelled. I proudly rattled off the gigs we had booked, ending with the Electric Banana in Pittsburgh.

"Oh yeah, the Electric Banana," Dr. Know laughed. "Look out for the owner, he don't like to pay. He pulled a gun on us."

We piled seven guys into my van: everybody in Hope plus Carco, keyboardist Jason Barkan, and David Kaufman, who was going to help drive. Our shows on the tour were sparsely attended—except for Friday night in Akron. That one was packed and felt great. Our last show was at the Electric Banana on Sunday. The owner was a fat guy wearing shades. He didn't pull a gun on us—but he didn't give us a dime, either.

"You didn't bring nobody," he shrugged. He did cough up the promised motel rooms, though. "Ask for John Genella," he grunted, handing me a ratty business card.

We drove to a really crappy motel and I asked for Mr. Genella. He stalked out in a cheap suit, looking like a cross between Lurch from *The Addams Family* and some low-level

Pittsburgh mafioso. Genella had big chompers and a raspy voice. "Where yer axes?" he growled, handing me the room keys. "Bring 'em in the back door. If ya don't like it, go to the Kings!"

I didn't know what he was talking about—until we drove past the even crappier Kings Motel on our way out of town the next day.

On the ride home, everybody passed out while Kaufman drove. I was sleeping through New Jersey in the backseat when he turned around, shook me awake, and said, "Hey, it's your turn."

We were going about sixty-five on Route 80. Kaufman jumped into the backseat. I grabbed the steering wheel and slid into the driver's seat. Carco was asleep on the passenger side. The red boom box leaning against the windshield was playing "Hitsville U.K." by the Clash. As soon as I sat down, the van started to shake, like when you're a kid riding your bike too fast down a hill and that front wheel starts trembling. I gripped the wheel with all my might, but I knew I'd already lost control.

"This is it! This is really it!" I shouted.

The van rolled three times. By some miracle, it landed upright in the shoulder lane. The U-Haul broke off, flipped over, skidded on its side, and screeched to a stop in front of the van. The windows were all shattered. There was blood everywhere. My nose was broken—shoved over to one side—and my face was cut up. I heard sirens, and the gruff voices of cops demanding to know what drugs we were on. I just lay there on the front seat in shock, until I was lifted into an ambulance. Nobody else was hurt. We were lucky to be alive.

In the ER, I kept asking Carco, "Do I look like Leon? I don't wanna look like Leon." Leon was our friend who had flown through a windshield during a car accident in New

Jersey. His face was badly disfigured. Leon went from being a cute, happy kid to a despondent drug addict who kept trying to kill himself. Poor Leon succeeded on his third try, jumping out a window at the Kenmore Hotel and landing on 23rd Street.

A doctor set my nose, but it healed crooked. My father wanted me to get it fixed. His insurance would pay for it, he said.

Meanwhile, my mother's health had taken a turn for the worse. She was on oxygen and pretty weak. "Please don't do this right now," she said, "I won't be able to take care of you." But my dad insisted, saying he really wanted to do this for me. I couldn't help thinking maybe he just didn't want a messed-up-looking son.

The night before my surgery, I stayed on the couch at his apartment in Edison, New Jersey. I was scared, and anxious about having to wake up at five a.m. My father sat down on the couch and got in my face all night: "What the fuck are ya doing with this music crap? Your mother had that dream. Her mother had that dream. They never went anywhere. You ain't never gonna make a dime. You better think about doing something else."

He drove me to the hospital in the morning. I was on no sleep. Waiting to be wheeled into the OR, all I could think about was the surgeon rebreaking my nose with a hammer, and my mother begging me not to do this.

I pulled off the hospital gown, threw on my clothes, and ran. My father was in the lobby when I came dashing out.

"You leave here, I'll never talk to you again!" he shouted.

He dropped me at a bus station without another word. I caught a bus to Port Authority, and took the subway downtown to Astor Place. I went into a phone booth, but I didn't know who to call. Lisa and I had been fighting, and my mother wasn't strong enough to deal with this. It was a cold gray morning. I felt like I had nobody in this world.

I went home to Queens, and told my mother I didn't do it.

"That's good," she whispered. She looked so tired when I bent over her bed to hug her.

I told my friends I didn't get my nose fixed because I was worried about it affecting my voice, but that wasn't the truth. My nose is still busted to this day.

I borrowed enough cash to buy another van, and got back to work. My days were long and late. After dropping off my last band, I'd meet friends for drinks at King Tut's Wah Wah Hut—which used to be A7—or at Lismar Lounge, a sleazy rocker hangout on First Avenue with skulls and crossbones on its black doors. I'd get home to Queens really late, and spend an hour trying to find a parking spot.

I would crawl into bed exhausted. But through the walls of my bedroom came horrifying choking sounds. My mother would be gasping for air, striving to clear the congestion that was drowning her. To this day, if any noise wakes me in the middle of the night, I panic.

Sometimes she cried, "Jesse! Jesse! Help! Help!" I'd drag myself out of bed, go sit by her side, and hold her hand for a few hours. She was so frightened about what was happening to her. She couldn't sleep because she was having nightmares about being buried alive in the dirt.

When I was little and had a nightmare, I would cry out, "Scared! Scared!" My mother always rushed in to soothe away my fears. Now, she needed me to comfort her. I played albums for her, like *Goodbye Yellow Brick Road*. I had her read the lyrics, because that calmed her down. I played Bruce Springsteen's monologues from his live albums. She liked hearing him talk about growing up in New Jersey.

It started to happen every night. I'd be passed out in bed and hear my name over and over. Sometimes I thought I was dreaming. Then I'd realize my mother was calling me.

I was so tired. *I can't handle this*, I would think. I began to dread it, and that made me feel guilty. But I still got up and went to her every time.

I met my father for dinner at a strip mall in Edison. Afterward, we walked to his car. He stopped, looked me square in the eye, and said, "Your mother's gonna die. And what are you kids gonna do when she does?"

"I think she's gonna live," I replied coolly, hiding how angry and scared his words made me feel.

I genuinely believed this, because even though she was so sick, my mother still had a tremendous fighting spirit. Once, she jumped out of bed and chased away her doctors. She'd been on oxygen for weeks, struggling to breathe, but she flew out of her bed screaming, "I'm not gonna die!" She chased them out of our apartment and down the hall.

I've since learned that people can have powerful bursts of energy shortly before they pass. But at the time, I was sure anyone who could run like that was probably going to outlive me.

Lisa hoped, too, that my mother would beat this thing. Lisa wrote, *I know that better things are on the way*—from a beautiful Kinks song—on a postcard and gave it to her. I still have it to this day.

But stress and exhaustion were taking a toll on me. I was always on edge, and Lisa and I kept breaking up and getting back together again. One cold January day, Lisa finally called it quits. "I have to move on," she said quietly. "I'm sorry."

I was furious. I felt so betrayed. How could she leave

me now? I didn't want to even try to remain friends. I really didn't handle it well.

To my surprise, my mother was upset about our breakup. As I sat by her side during more frightening nights, she'd murmur, "Get back with Lisa. Please get back with her."

"I wish I could," I'd say.

My mother died in the hospital during a stifling heat wave in late May of 1986. When I'd visited her that afternoon, I had a bad feeling. I went out drinking alone at Alcatraz on Avenue A. As I sat at the bar trying to cool off, Neil Young's haunting song "Helpless" came on.

When he sang, "*The chains are locked and tied across the door,*" I just knew.

I got home, very drunk, at five in the morning. When I walked in, Papa Artie and Uncle Jon jumped up from the couch. Neither of them drank often, but I could smell liquor on their breath.

"Your mother's gone," Papa Artie said.

I burst into tears and went to my room.

Chapter 21

Alphabet Soup

It was a long time ago
When I let that arrow go
—"The Archer"

After Lisa and I broke up for the final time, followed by my mother dying, I felt lost and alone. But I just kept going. I had to figure out how to support myself and Juliet. I redoubled my efforts to become a round-the-clock Man with Van. Like Travis Bickle says in *Taxi Driver*: "Anytime, anywhere."

In between van jobs, Carco and I wandered around downtown putting up fliers to get more van jobs. One hot July day, we were walking up Second Avenue when I noticed a striking blond girl with lively brown eyes, wearing white Doc Martens and a patent-vinyl miniskirt. She was sitting on a stoop with a girl I'd gone out with a couple times. It would have been awkward to try to talk to her then, so I just waved.

After Lisa and I broke up, I tried dating a few girls. But with my mother slipping away before my eyes, I couldn't connect with anyone. I felt numb. I didn't believe I'd ever meet anyone again who could love me like Lisa had—or someone I might love as much.

A few nights later, I went to see the Bad Brains and Living Colour at the Roxy. Living Colour was a new all-Black rock band blowing up while the Bad Brains were self-destructing.

Island Records founder Chris Blackwell wanted to sign the Bad Brains and put them on tour with U2. When the Bad Brains met with Blackwell, though, H.R. said to him, "You killed Bob Marley," and walked out on the deal.

Leaving the Roxy, I spotted that girl again in those white Doc Martens and a tight Jack Daniel's T-shirt that really showed off her voluptuous figure. This time, I got up the nerve to talk to her. Her name was Alyssa Wendt. I danced all the way home after getting her number. It was the first time I had felt excited about anything in months.

I invited her to come see Vinny and Jae's band A.P.P.L.E. play at Tin Pan Alley. This narrow bar was right across from the Brill Building on 49th and Broadway, where songwriters like Carole King and Doc Pomus wrote big hits in the early sixties. Tin Pan Alley was run by lesbian activists who fed the bands and paid them well. But before they would book your band, they had to read your lyrics. Vinny loved that.

After the show, Alyssa and I went for a walk on Eighth Avenue. It was July 4 and the city was dead. Even Times Square was eerily quiet. We wandered through deserted parking garages in the heat, and talked for hours. She smelled like tea rose perfume and the promise of summer.

She was seventeen and I was twenty. Three years is nothing when you get older, but at first Alyssa seemed so young to me. As we talked, though, I found out she was very smart and funny, and knew a great deal about art and photography. The sparkle in her eyes reminded me a bit of my mother.

Alyssa's father was an architect and her mother was a painter. They were divorced and she was their only child. We hung out at her father's apartment on East 9th Street. Now, instead of sweating on some stoop, I was looking down at my world from an air-conditioned high-rise, drinking her dad's cold beer.

Alyssa had come from Phoenix to attend NYU as a photography major. She showed me pictures she had taken. They were great. She had an artist's eye; it was in her DNA. She made me mixtapes with stuff I'd never heard before: Hawkwind, J. Geils, Blue Cheer. She wasn't stuck in the punk-rock box with what she listened to or how she dressed. Some of my friends, like Matt Zombie, had already fallen for her. She was the new hot girl everybody wanted.

Alyssa's father was German and had survived World War II as a teenager. Years later, his life was saved by a Jewish doctor in New York. Alyssa's dad liked me and would take us out for gourmet veggie burgers and crisp white wine at Spring Street Natural. My father and I were barely speaking. Having Alyssa's dad be so nice felt good.

Alyssa's mother wasn't quite as friendly. I probably didn't look too promising to her with my dreadlocks and rusty van. Lisa would give me and Alyssa the skunk eye whenever she saw us.

Alyssa liked coming with me and Carco on van jobs and meeting all the crazy bands. She had a hunger for adventure and the wildness of New York after dark. She always came out to see Hope play, too. After shows or van jobs, Alyssa would return home with me to Whitestone. I felt safe sleeping next to her there. She brought life into that apartment, after so much sadness.

When classes began, Alyssa moved into the dorms. For me, it was like traveling back in time, hanging around the campus and sneaking into the cafeteria again. She began leaving town, though, pretty often. She would fly home to Scottsdale, or to Europe during breaks. I was constantly pulling out of the airport with tears in my eyes. It seemed like she was always leaving and I was always crying. Like Lenny Bruce said, people don't stay.

Alyssa sent me postcards, but seeing the beautiful places she got to explore while I was stuck rattling around the city in my van almost made it worse. The fact that she was able to travel, and had parents who cared, made me feel broke and pathetic. Then she'd come home and we'd be so happy at first. But Alyssa loved to party, and if some band she liked came to town, she might disappear with her friends for days. I would chase her around, trying to get her back. I was losing myself and any mojo I'd ever had.

Meanwhile, I did the same thing my dad always did—obsessed about the ex-girlfriend in front of the new girlfriend, making her feel insecure. I couldn't stop myself from talking about Lisa. Deep down, I probably wasn't any more ready to commit than Alyssa was.

Guys flirted pretty aggressively with her everywhere we went. One afternoon we were hanging out on a bench in Tompkins Square after a hardcore matinee at the bandshell. This creepy hippie with long dirty-blond hair, a matted beard, and crazy Charles Manson eyes came up to us and stood staring at Alyssa's chest. I'd seen him wandering around the park before, with a rooster tucked under his filthy jean jacket, selling weed. His name was Daniel Rakowitz but everybody called him the Chicken Man.

We got up and walked away, but he followed us, getting in Alyssa's face. I was about to shove him when he drifted off, muttering angrily to himself. I was used to nuts like him roaming around Tompkins, and unhoused people sleeping on the lawns and in the bandshell at night. The park never closed, which attracted people afraid of the city's dirty, crowded shelters.

The Lower East Side was rapidly gentrifying, though, and the yuppies wanted the park cleaned up. I saw tanks rolling down Avenue B, heading toward Tompkins Square.

Tension was building. The mayor ordered the police to remove the unhoused and enforce a one a.m. curfew. In protest, two hundred people marched down Avenue A on a muggy August night. They were met by four hundred cops. Police on horseback clubbed the demonstrators, while cops in riot gear rushed them from inside the park. The commander was forced to resign when photos of bloodied, beaten New Yorkers hit the front pages and the TV news.

One year later, the Chicken Man brought a big pot of soup to the park's free-food line. After people ate the soup, he went around bragging that it contained pieces of his dead girlfriend. Nobody believed him, since he was always saying weird stuff. Stephan, who had moved to Rakowitz's building on 9th and C, scrawled on the guy's door, as a joke, *She drives me crazy!* from the Fine Young Cannibals song, and *Is it soup yet?* Rakowitz's girlfriend, Monika Beerle, was a Swiss modern-dance student who worked at Billy's Topless. She hadn't been around much lately, and her friends thought she was in Switzerland visiting her family.

A month later, the FBI banged on Stephan's door. The police had arrested Rakowitz, who confessed to murdering Monika, dismembering her body in their clawfoot bathtub, and boiling the flesh off her bones. He told them he was a cannibal and led them to a storage locker at the Port Authority Bus Terminal filled with Monika's bones and a bunch of kitty litter. Rakowitz was found not guilty by reason of insanity, and committed to a psych ward for the criminally insane. The FBI cleared Stephan, who told me he felt terrible when he learned that Rakowitz's ravings had actually been true. A chill ran through me when I realized how close the Chicken Man had gotten to Alyssa.

When her semester ended, Alyssa left to spend the summer in

San Francisco. I wasn't happy about this, but we were still in love and I figured we'd be okay.

I got a second job working the door at King Tut's Wah Wah Hut. I wanted a clean slate for the summer so I shaved my head. It felt good to get rid of my matted dreads and feel the breeze on my scalp. I put on a suit and a fedora, and ran the door with Stan the bouncer, who checked IDs and sold coke. Stan was a stocky thirty-something Black guy who lived in the projects on Avenue D. He knew everybody in the neighborhood, from the addicts to the artists. I stamped hands, collected money, and ran the door while Stan was in back doing his deals.

During the lulls, Stan and I chatted about the new Batman movie, or some shooting that had happened in the neighborhood. We became friends. I've had many menial jobs: gas station attendant, dishwasher, dog walker, snow shoveler, janitor, foot messenger, telemarketer. I learned that you can always find common ground with someone—even if you're from different planets and would probably never cross paths if it weren't for the job. Working together breaks all that down. Kind of like jail.

I met lots of cute girls at the Wah Wah Hut, but I stayed faithful to Alyssa. We wrote each other love letters and sent postcards back and forth all summer. I worked day and night, but still couldn't cover the rent on the Whitestone apartment. It was too expensive, and too painful to be there, anyway.

Carco's parents were kicking him out and moving to Pennsylvania. We found a cheap ground-floor apartment in Greenpoint near the Vespoles, right across from St. Cecilia's Church. The place had three bedrooms—for me, Carco, and Juliet—and the Sunshine Diner was down the street. I took that as a good omen, after the darkness Juliet and I had come through.

Watching all the weddings and funerals at St. Cecilia's was like watching a movie. There's nothing like waking up hungover as hell and seeing a coffin slide into a hearse. Carco and I started calling each other "Stiff": "Hey, Stiff, pass the orange juice."

When Alyssa came back, she moved into my room with a pile of suitcases—and an envelope full of photos she had taken in California. Some were of shirtless boys lying on her futon. We had a huge fight, and I went crazy and trashed my room. I was crushed that I had been loyal to her while she was hanging out with hot guys—and documenting it.

Looking back, my grief had probably made me hold on too tight to a young woman who needed to be free to explore who she was. But for me, it was the last straw. I swore to myself that I would never give it all to anyone again. I would always hold something back.

Chapter 22

The Green Door

*We were the children who needed those dreams the worst
We asked for God but all they had left was church*
—"About You"

The Greenpoint apartment was always full of friends. British guitarist Rick Bacchus, aka the Atomic Elf, flopped on our couch. He was a warm-hearted guy, always fun to have around. Another wild Queens boy, Victor Murgatroyd—who had no job and nowhere to live—crashed at our place, too, sometimes. Whenever we were broke, which was often, Victor would say, "There's ways, boys! There's ways!" Victor got us into clubs for free, and scrounged free drinks. If a bill was due, he'd find something to sell, or a girl to pay it. Eventually, Victor became a big music executive working for Clive Davis. I guess there's ways!

Funny enough, St. Cecilia is the patron saint of musicians. I like to think she was watching over us.

This desolate neighborhood became our home. We lived on supermarket spaghetti and Driggs Pizza. We found a few other misfits in Greenpoint and Williamsburg. It only made sense to throw some house parties. I met girls at those parties and at clubs. I got pretty good at charming them into my bedroom. But I didn't like anyone spending the night. After Alyssa and I broke up, I was hell-bent on staying single. I didn't ever want to hurt like that again.

My friends called my bed "the ejector mattress," because

I would come up with any remotely believable excuse to get a woman out after we'd been together. I'd offer to drive her home, or pretend that I had to go pick up a band at three a.m. I just couldn't deal with sleeping next to anyone. It felt even more intimate than having sex.

I had lots of van jobs at the Music Building in Midtown. The place had very few working toilets; bands pissed in the sinks. Madonna lived there before she made it big, in a room where the Freaks rehearsed now. The Freaks were long-haired weirdos who played "heavy Orange rock" through big Orange amps. They gigged with bands like Soundgarden and Raging Slab.

The first time I picked up the Freaks, they climbed into my backseat droning on in the weirdest voices I'd ever heard, like a record on the wrong speed. I turned around and there was that Whitestone legend Howie Pyro.

I almost didn't recognize him. The sharp teenage bassist for the Blessed was heavier now, with long black hair and a thick goatee. He wore a leather motorcycle vest and silver skull rings on every finger. He was married to Freaks singer Andrea Matthews. They lived near me in Greenpoint, so Howie and I started hanging out. We bonded over *Underdog* cartoons, Iggy and the Stooges, and *The Three Stooges*. We loved driving around Brooklyn in my van, and if we happened to pass some fly-by-night carnival, we couldn't resist jumping on the rides. That freaked Vinny Vespole out.

"Just picture the greasy guy putting that together with a wrench. Just picture him!" Vinny cried.

On summer Sundays, Howie and I would pull up in front of Sidewalk Café on Avenue A and pile a bunch of crazy rockers, hungover barflies, and night birds into my van. We'd drive out to Coney Island with a little boom box blaring, and hit the wildest rides—the Zipper, the Hellhole, the Thunderbolt, the Brooklyn Barge. If we saw puke on the floor, we knew it was a good one.

Coney Island was still pretty sketchy, but it made me happy that I was running around the same boardwalk where Papa Artie had goofed around with his friends, or kissed a girl. I took dates out there, too. Walking on the beach on a hot summer night and looking back at the Wonder Wheel and the glowing lights of Astroland felt so romantic.

After as many rides as we could stomach, my friends and I would run down to the pier and dive into the ocean in our clothes, without a care that we might break our necks on the shopping carts, concrete chunks, and rocks lurking beneath the surface. Then we'd rush back to my van and maybe swing by Nathan's on Surf Avenue for fries before heading back to Manhattan.

Dee Dee Ramone came with us once, and rode the old wood-track Cyclone coaster—which had escaped demolition after all. I turned around and laughed at Howie and Dee Dee screaming in the car behind me. Coney Island was our poor man's vacation: a holiday in the city.

Howie was an obsessive collector of pop-culture weirdness. He hoarded rare vinyl, freaky toys, fetish magazines, comic books, and VHS tapes of monster movies. If you asked Howie about some oddity, he'd loudly exclaim, "Oh, I have that!" and start pawing through his collection. He could never find it.

Howie and Andrea had mostly been in same-sex relationships before they met, but Howie didn't see himself as gay or straight. He loved everyone. The music scene seemed so free, but it was actually pretty homophobic, and I think Howie struggled with that. He covered up his pain with his charm, his collecting, and, at times, with drugs.

When Andrea and Howie split up, he moved in with me, Carco, and Juliet. It took three days to pack and move all Howie's stuff. I finally passed out cold in the hallway, with his boxes tumbling over me.

We had lots of fun movie nights and wild parties. The cartoonist Ed "Big Daddy" Roth asked Howie to write his biography. That was a big deal for Howie, and he took it seriously. Howie was a couch guy. He wrote on the couch, smoking cigarettes, and fell asleep on the couch in his sweatpants with the TV blaring. I'd come home from a crazy night driving bands around, or a date that had left me feeling lonely and confused, and Howie would be there on the couch. I'd tell him all my problems. We'd laugh, and then I wouldn't feel so bad.

Howie grounded me. He brought me comfort, like a mom or an older brother. He was *"my best friend, my doctor,"* like Dylan sang in "Just Like Tom Thumb's Blues." I called him "Doctor Howard." We loved it when the Three Stooges shook each other's hands real fast: "Doctor Fein, Doctor Howard, Doctor Fein, Doctor Howard." That cracked us up.

Howie could get along with anybody. He was friends with Johnny *and* Joey Ramone, who hated each other. Skinheads, Hells Angels, drag queens, comic-book nerds, fashionistas—they all loved Howie. Maybe it was the deep empathy in those green eyes. Juliet was a shy girl who loved the *Grease* soundtrack and Tennessee Williams. She was uneasy at our raucous parties sometimes—but she could always lock eyes with Howie and feel safe.

By 1990 I was fed up with trying to get Hope off the ground. I hated the music that was big at the time: grunge and jock funk. I missed the dirty decadence and great pop songs of the

1970s. I wanted a band that was a gang; that played aggressive music and looked cool.

"Let's do something just for fun," I told Howie one night. "Let's make the band we'd love to go see. I won't play guitar and be so serious. I'll take my shirt off and make my hair all crazy and jump around like an idiot. And you're gonna shave that fucking beard."

We put a band together that was a five-headed monster: Rick Bacchus and Danny on guitar, Michael on drums, Howie on bass, and me on vocals. We were best friends with tons of drive and personality, determined to be the wildest band in town. We just needed a name.

I started riffing on the Lenny Bruce joke: "Dad, what's a degenerate?" Howie dug into a pile and emerged with an old movie poster: *The Degeneration*. He pulled out a vintage photo of a sexy blonde. Howie and Michael pasted *D Generation* over her eyes for our logo.

We wrote D Generation's first song, "No Way Out," in our apartment. It was a raw, fast rocker with a catchy chorus and me spewing as many words as I could about everything I hated:

All the rubbish that you cherish
With your hedonistic pleasures
And your latest status symbols
Just can't stay

Seen the majors chase the minors
With the military blinders
Dangle carrots in the faces
Of the USA

Being brothers, Danny and Michael had this telepathic musical connection. They could play the Who's entire *Live at Leeds* album together without even looking at each other, or bust out perfect harmonies on some Beatles song in a taxi. At thirty, Howie was "the old guy." The rest of us thought he was ancient. Probably because Howie's favorite word was "ouch." If you said your back hurt, Howie would moan, "Ohhhh, you don't knooow . . . my back is soooo much worse." He was like Al Pacino in *Dog Day Afternoon*: "I'm dyin' here!"

But Howie was also very handsome, especially after he shaved off that biker beard and cut his hair. With his high cheekbones and sharp jawline, Howie never took a bad picture. Photographers like Francesco Scavullo and David Godlis loved to shoot him. Howie's favorite was the Godlis photo of him and the Blessed's guitarist cutting each other's hair with a BIC lighter in a Bowery flophouse.

My dreads had grown back, so I added hair extensions and spiked them up with Krazy Glue. We wrote more tough, snotty songs, and rehearsed at Giorgio's. We played the first D Generation gig there to a sold-out sweathouse of the coolest kids we could find to invite. We exploded onto the stage like we'd been shot from a cannon—with the pent-up rage and frustration of our entire lives—and left it a pile of broken gear. I was picking confetti out of my hair for weeks.

On New Year's Eve, my friends and I threw the first Green Door party at Giorgio's. We named it after his building's green door—not the seventies porno flick. Howie and Lisa were going to DJ; Victor ran all over town inviting everyone he'd ever met; and Carco had big plans to hang out and drink for free.

Lisa and I had gotten past our breakup and become friends again. I understood now that she had left me to save herself.

"I got so mad because you broke up with me at such a bad time," I said, when we finally talked it out.

"I was seeing a therapist," Lisa explained. "She said because we were going back and forth so much, we probably needed to break up."

"That was probably true," I admitted.

"But I told her," Lisa continued, "'Enid's gonna die. I should move in with Jesse and help him raise Juliet.' My therapist just said, 'Or not.' That was the first time I even realized I had a choice."

That's when I got it. Lisa couldn't take on that heavy burden at such a young age. She had her own life to live, and we had gone as far as we could. Eventually, Alyssa and I became friends again, too, before she moved out to San Francisco for good.

Lisa was a great DJ. Her upbeat energy and big smile were infectious. She dressed up in tight sparkly outfits, and really got the crowd going as she danced behind the turntables. Howie was a hit, too, playing everything from Funkadelic to the Cramps. His musical knowledge was deep. More than any of us, Howie understood how influential Giorgio really was.

Our first Green Door party was packed, raging until six in the morning. We made lots of cash for ourselves and for Giorgio. "Do it again!" our friends begged, so we did, one month later. We gave Giorgio a bottle of Johnnie Walker. He sat in a corner sipping his scotch while people danced themselves into joyful oblivion. After midnight, Giorgio took the bottle up to his loft, with the party still going full blast. He came down again around four a.m., full of drunken enthusiasm. "Jesseee," he slurred, wrapping an arm around me like a friendly bear, "let's take this fantastic event around the world. Call me tomorrow. We'll get an omelet and have a real chat. This is only the beginning!"

Giorgio made us return the next morning to clean his place thoroughly. It was disgusting—and we were hungover and burnt as hell—but we did as he asked. It was a good lesson for us. We were also motivated by all the money we found on the floor.

After cleaning up, I was starving for that omelet. I called Giorgio. "Who is this?" Giorgio shouted over the phone. "Omelet? Are you crazy?" He had no idea why I was waking him up. I had to laugh. It took until the evening for Giorgio to become a nice guy again.

We started throwing Green Door parties every two weeks. We quickly outgrew Giorgio's and moved to Boy Bar at 15 St. Marks, where drag queens like Miss Guy and Lipsynka performed. I was making enough money to cover the bills without having to lug sofas up tenement stairs anymore. This is how we made things happen. This is how we made our lives.

Boy Bar's landlord was Paul McGregor, the hairstylist who gave Jane Fonda her shag for *Klute*. He had curly brown hair and a big handlebar mustache. People lined up along St. Marks to get a haircut from Paul, who'd roller-skate into his salon dressed as a cowboy, a Native American, or maybe a pirate. He'd swoop into our parties, back from Fire Island or Bali all tan and muscular, stinking of garlic and booze.

I would have sworn Paul was gay. "Oh no, Paul likes the ladies," Bob Gruen told me. "Warren Beatty's character in *Shampoo* was actually based on him."

I loved that shop owners like Paul, Bleecker Bob, and Tish and Snooky from Manic Panic were just as outrageous as their customers. They showed me you could build a life on your own terms, and not give a fuck what anybody else thought.

Gruen was a renowned music photographer. He brought Joe Strummer to the Green Door one night. My cousin Matt was DJing and happened to be playing one of Joe's solo records right as he walked in.

"This is one of the D Generation guys!" Bob shouted, bringing Joe over to me. I was thrilled. A few years back, Carco and I had snuck into Joe's sound check at the Palladium. He let us stay while he taught his band a new song, and even put us on the list for the show. Jack Flanagan was a bouncer at the Palladium at that time, so we figured he could get us backstage to hang out with Joe some more. But Carco got bombed and started calling Jack a big fat red lobster. Jack got fed up and tossed our asses out.

At Boy Bar, though, Joe and I talked for hours over many shots of tequila. I grilled him about the movies the Clash watched when they were becoming a band. I asked a million questions about the songs.

Joe had the patience of a saint. Before we knew it, the sun was coming up. I couldn't believe how kind Strummer was, and how much of himself he gave.

Chapter 23

I Got Something for You Boys

Dressed up like each other's dream
We were kinda killers
—"She Don't Love Me Now"

D Generation really was a band that was a gang. We ran around together every night in leather jackets, stovepipe pants, and Creepers, talking up our shows. With our black eyeliner and spiked-up hair, we stuck out like five sore thumbs in the era of grunge—and that was the point.

Grunge had beaten the style out of rock and roll. Even New York bands were wearing cargo shorts and flannel shirts like Seattle dads heading out to mow the lawn. We wanted people to know, the moment they saw us, that we were something different. They might laugh at us, but they would know.

Before we ever dreamed of a record deal, we wanted a bar deal. Once we could drink for free at our favorite bars downtown, we felt like we had made it. Labels weren't signing bands from New York, anyway.

D Generation was also a dysfunctional family, with two wild brothers—Danny and Michael—often at each other's throats. Howie and Rick had been briefly involved, adding fuel to the fire. And, like most lead singers, I could be an insecure control freak. We brought all that onstage, which made D Generation pretty compelling. Sometimes we hated each other, but then we'd play a great gig and be in love again.

We played regularly at Continental, a Third Avenue dive

popular for its earsplitting sound system and cheap drinks. Roger, the manager, loved it when Rick poured rum down the bar and lit it on fire, or I jumped off the stage onto the wobbly little tables and sent beer bottles and drinks flying. As long as we packed the place, we could do whatever the hell we wanted and Trigger, the owner, would generously pay us a thousand bucks.

Producer Daniel Rey brought Joey Ramone to see us at Continental, which was catty-corner from Joey's apartment. I was thrilled when I saw Joey towering over the crowd. I felt so happy when he said he loved the show, but too embarrassed to tell him I was that twelve-year-old kid who used to call him up.

A tall, androgynous blonde named Marti began photographing D Generation shows. She was this beautiful creature who sprawled on the floor with her long legs in the air, or climbed on top of the bar, to get the shots she wanted. And she never stopped dancing.

Marti and I hung out a lot at her apartment above an Indian restaurant on First Avenue, watching Cassavetes movies and listening to Lenny Bruce and Otis Redding. We all fell in love with Marti, and she fell in love with us. She was at every gig, and got every joke. She became D Gen's sixth member, only instead of a guitar around her neck, she had her camera.

Marti was also a talented actress/performance artist who wore leather and carried a whip—even though she had the softest voice and the sweetest heart. We went to see her perform in late-night plays at Jackie 60, the Tuesday-night party at a little club in the Meatpacking District. Drag queens, punks, leather daddies, latex lovers, and sex workers mingled with Stephen Sprouse and Debbie Harry while Kitty Boots ran the door, keeping out the stiffs. We'd walk in, and the MC would campily announce over booming techno: "D Generation in the house."

Our new friends from Jackie 60 came to our gigs, and some made their way into our songs. This raw, decadent scene crossed all the lines—gay, straight, trans—nobody cared. This was why we lived in New York, and why we loved it.

After another crazy show at Continental, I left around five a.m. with Howie and a cute girl. We were walking to my van when Howie mumbled, "I gotta get some cigarettes."

"Ah, c'mon, man," I said, "let's just go home."

Howie ignored me and staggered toward the deli on the corner.

"Meet us at the van!" I yelled.

I walked the girl down to my van and we got inside. Suddenly, there was loud pounding on its metal sides. I grabbed my crowbar from under the driver's seat and jumped out, hopped up on alcohol and machismo.

Instantly, I was surrounded by six little teenagers. I raised the crowbar, hoping to scare them off, but a kid behind me snatched it out of my hand. He tossed it to the guy standing in front of me, who swung it hard into my knee, shouting, "Take that, motherfucker!" Then he smashed it into my leg again. I fell down, afraid I was about to be beaten to death with my own crowbar.

At that moment, Howie came out of the deli with his cigarettes and clocked what was happening. By some miracle, he spotted a police car cruising up Third Avenue. Howie ran into the middle of the street and flagged it down. The cops made a quick U-turn and sped toward me the wrong way with lights flashing. The kid dropped the crowbar and ran off with his friends.

Howie hauled me up off the ground with a grin and said, "You pull out a knife, you get stabbed."

* * *

A young A&R exec named Debbie Southwood-Smith saw D Generation at Continental. Debbie loved punk and cool, sleazy rock and roll. She totally got us, and set up a meeting with EMI Records president Daniel Glass.

We lived our lives mostly at night, below 14th Street. Taking the subway uptown to EMI's office on a sunny morning felt like traveling to another planet. Daniel's receptionist showed us around the office and invited us to pick out some complimentary CDs. We lunged at them like hungry jackals, grabbing handfuls of Jethro Tull and Billy Idol discs and stuffing them into manila envelopes while she smiled nervously.

Meeting Daniel was an instant love connection. He was a skinny Jewish guy with tight curly hair, big blue eyes, and a great smile. Like us, Daniel hung out and DJ'd at Jackie 60 and Don Hill's. Yet he also reminded us of our nutty relatives back in Queens. Daniel had their warmth and raunchy sense of humor.

We felt safe with Daniel, and understood, so we signed with EMI Chrysalis a few weeks later in Continental's dirty dressing room, over Jägermeister and champagne provided by Roger. Right after that first meeting, though, I raced the other guys down to a used record store on 8th Street to try to sell my Jethro Tull CDs.

We were thrilled to get a record deal . . . but the wheels at a major label grind slowly. We got bored sitting around waiting to go into the studio to record our first album.

A small indie label in California had put out a seven-inch single for us before we signed to EMI. So we figured, *Let's go to LA and see if anybody outside of New York even likes us.* I booked three gigs and we flew west on $99 plane tickets I found in the *Village Voice*.

I loved seeing the palm trees and sunshine as we taxied

down the runway at LAX. Los Angeles looked beautiful already.

Reality was different. TV shows make Hollywood look so shiny and clean, but up close it was decayed and crumbling, with funky old buildings that hadn't seen fresh paint since the 1940s. But I could still picture Humphrey Bogart strolling into Terner's Liquor on Sunset, and Marilyn Monroe having dinner at Musso & Frank. We drove past the Hacienda Motel where Sam Cooke was shot, with its battered old sign offering *Daily Rates and Kitchenettes.*

In New York, real estate is so limited that history gets rolled over by relentless new development. LA spreads out, with this creepy underbelly of sex and murder that feels like it has been around forever.

We checked into the Regency Suites on Hollywood Boulevard, where a lot of bands stayed. Porno film crews were all over the hotel, shooting scenes in the rooms and even out by the pool. The Lower East Side was dangerous and fucked up, but Hollywood reeked of quiet desperation. In New York, we threw our own shows and made our own luck. If you're the most beautiful or talented person in your high school and you head to Hollywood, you're seeking the kind of fame that can only be doled out by the industry. And it doesn't always happen.

The aftershock of all those shattered dreams was right there on the streets. Sex was for sale all day long, out in the open. Hookers strolled the parking lots and strip malls. Male hustlers cruised the burger joints and bus stops on Santa Monica Boulevard. New York can break you, but it's up front about it. It doesn't dangle starry promises of fame while it's screwing you.

Our first show was at Club Lingerie on Sunset Boulevard. When we arrived for sound check, the place was dark. There was nobody around except one guy drinking at the bar. He was thin as a blade with thick reddish-blond hair, dressed in head-to-toe black.

He stood up and grunted, "Sticca. Lemme give you guys a hand." I'd heard of this guy. Michael Sticca was the legendary roadie for the New York Dolls, Blondie, and the Dead Boys.

Sticca marched out of the club and started unloading our rental van. Meanwhile, the club's manager emerged long enough to tell us we weren't getting a sound check. Sticca marched back into the club and got us a sound check. Meanwhile, our drummer Michael was on a pay phone having some long-distance drama with his girlfriend. Sticca walked over, got on the phone with her, and straightened everything out.

The show itself was pretty fantastic. All kinds of Hollywood freaks, punks, and rockers came out, dressed to the nines, and they loved us.

Afterward, Sticca helped us load our gear back into the van. We thanked him and tried to pay him, but he wouldn't take a dime. "I'll see ya soon," was all he said.

Our next show was at the Roxy, where scenes from *Rock 'n' Roll High School* were filmed. When we pulled into the parking lot, a tall old guy wearing a pink suit and weird sunglasses strolled over to us. "Heyyy," he said in a nasally whine, "you guys are D Generation. And I'm Kim Fowley." Fowley was the producer who had put the Runaways together, and written songs for KISS and the Dead Boys. Years later, the Runaways's bass player accused him of drugging and raping her at a party when she was sixteen.

Inside the club was a card from MC5 guitarist Wayne Kramer welcoming us to LA. Once again, the audience was outrageous, fun, and wild. We invited the whole crowd back to the Regency and threw a Green Door–style party, blasting our mixtapes on a boom box. People were dancing on the beds, jumping in the pool, and going crazy until the sun came up.

The next afternoon, we set off to get breakfast at the Denny's on Sunset to ease our hangovers. We figured we'd grab a cab, but that wasn't really a thing in LA. So we walked, baking in the sun in our black New York clothes, with people honking and staring at us from their cars like we were aliens.

Our gig the next night fell through, so I called up Joe Sib, the singer for Wax, an LA band that had played with D Generation a few times at Continental. Joe came up through the hardcore scene and had the same hyper let's-make-something-happen energy as I had. I always knew that if I were ever in trouble in California, he would be the guy to call. "I got a spot," Joe said on the phone. "Bar Deluxe. I DJ there sometimes. The second floor would be perfect. Well, there's no stage. But I'll build one. And the floorboards are missing. But fuck it, I can fix that. You guys just show up. We'll make it happen."

Bar Deluxe was a small club on a dodgy corner of Las Palmas, near the porno theaters. Joe and a buddy of his carted a bunch of wood up to the second floor and spent the whole day nailing down floorboards, building a stage, and setting up a PA. Meanwhile, we made fliers at Kinko's and put them up all over the neighborhood. That turned out to be the best gig of the whole trip. I'd always heard that "gig" stood for "get it going," and Joe Sib sure did.

We threw another after-party and this time the hotel called the cops, who shut the whole thing down. The next day, we moved to the Hyatt on Sunset—the legendary Riot House where bands like Led Zeppelin and the Who raised hell in their heyday. Now it was just another boring hotel.

After we checked in, I went out on my balcony on the fifteenth floor and yelled down to Michael, whose room was one floor below mine. He walked onto his balcony, climbed over the railing, and hung by his hands, dangling over Sunset Boulevard, grinning up at me. Horrified, I held my breath until he pulled himself back up to safety. "What the fuck were you thinking?" I yelled. He just laughed.

The next morning, Rick and I got in the elevator to head down to the lobby. The rest of the guys were waiting by the van that was taking us to the airport. The elevator stopped at the second floor, and in walked Little Richard, the man who invented rock and roll. He stepped inside wearing black trousers, a black silk shirt, sunglasses, and a thin layer of pancake makeup.

"Hi, boys," he said, flashing that dazzling smile, "what band are you in?"

"D Generation!" I replied.

"I heard of you guys. I heard of you," he said, bobbing his head.

When we reached the lobby, Little Richard sashayed out the door and into a waiting black town car. Rick and I ran to the van to tell the other guys. "We just met Little Richard!" I shouted. "This is incredible!"

Just then, that black town car pulled up beside our van. The backseat window rolled down and there was Little Richard again. "Hey, come over here, D Generation," he called out, "I got something for you boys."

I ran to the window, and he handed me four small books. "Wow, thank you," I said.

Little Richard winked, and the town car pulled away. I stood looking after it, dumbstruck. Then I looked down at the books. They were Christian paperbacks about God and Jesus, each one signed by Little Richard.

We flew home pretty burnt, but feeling really optimistic, blessed by the King of Rock and Roll.

Chapter 24

Coney Island High

*All my friends down rabbit holes
Thick as thieves, don't know what we stole*
—"Queens of A"

D Generation had recorded a few demos at Electric Lady Studios with our friend Adam Yellin, who snuck us in after hours. Now, we proudly strutted through the door as major-label artists to record our first album with producer David Bianco.

D Generation came out with a bang: full-page raves in *Rolling Stone* and *SPIN,* and a color photo spread in the *New York Times.* Our publicist, Garvey Rich, constantly egged me on to break bottles, get into fights, and take my clothes off onstage so he could get us into Page Six, the *New York Post* gossip column. This was right up my alley, as you can imagine. "Jesse, you and Danny go in that restaurant and drag the tables out into the street!" Garvey would shout. "It'll get a great write-up!"

At the Ritz, I hopped on top of the fancy grand piano set up onstage for a band that Joan Jett's manager, Kenny Laguna, was handling. I danced all over it like a nut. Laguna ran after me screaming bloody murder, and I got tossed out on my ass by some Hells Angels. That made Page Six, too.

Our first single, "No Way Out," was blowing up on FM radio. Then Daniel Glass left EMI and his replacement wasn't a fan. Reportedly, EMI's plugger called the radio stations and said: "Stop playing D Generation. Play Queensrÿche."

The fix was in. EMI dropped us.

Everything stopped. It was pretty grim. We all felt depressed and beaten down. I figured I'd be schlepping sofas again real soon, or selling shoes at Trash and Vaudeville.

Our tour was already booked, though, so we said screw it, let's go. We squeezed into a rental van and played gigs from Akron to Jacksonville, laughing at America as it passed by our windows. As broke as we were, that tour brought us closer together than ever.

When we got back to New York, Garvey said, "You're gonna get another deal."

"Are you crazy?" I scoffed. "It's over."

"Just watch," he said.

Debbie Southwood-Smith was with A&M Records in Los Angeles now, and she wanted us. A bidding war broke out between A&M, Virgin, and Columbia Records. D Generation was flown around the country for fancy dinners with record executives. We were getting fat from all the booze and sushi.

We loved Debbie, but we went with Columbia because it was in New York, and we'd all grown up staring at that classic red label spinning around our turntables. Columbia offered us the most money it had ever paid for an unknown band. Because we were cocky little fucks, we said, "We'll sign . . . if you come to Coney Island and ride the Cyclone with us."

On a drizzly April day, we piled into a limo with label president Don Ienner and some other suits. It was the offseason, but Astroland opened the roller coaster for us. There's nothing scarier than that first steep climb up the Cyclone's bumpy wooden ramp, and the terrifying moment when you're perched at the top with a spectacular view of the Atlantic Ocean, knowing you're about to drop like a stone. Everybody screamed as we flew down that first drop, and the next one and the next.

I relished putting some record executives through that. When we rattled to a halt, we signed the contract and then headed back to Manhattan to get drunk.

We met with a bunch of producers, and settled on Ric Ocasek from the Cars. Ric had produced hit songs, but had also made a Bad Brains album. We figured he could handle us.

Recording with Ric was wonderful. He worked fast, yet he was soft-spoken and very encouraging in the studio. Our songs sounded so big, but still raw and alive. I invited Joey Ramone to come by the studio one day to see who was taller.

"People on the street think I'm you!" Joey exclaimed.

"Oh yeah? People think I'm you," Ric said.

They stood back to back. Joey had about two inches on Ric.

I was looking for some way to kick our song "Frankie" up a notch in the studio. It was inspired by Skel Vespole's cross-dressing, and the stigma he endured.

Hope had opened for Alan Vega's electro-punk duo Suicide at CBGB on a steamy August night back in 1986. Alan had strutted onstage like a sharp punk Elvis in a white fringed leather jacket, white polyester bell bottoms, and a white headband wrapped around his wild shock of jet-black hair. Alan screamed like he was having a nervous breakdown, while Martin Rev pushed his synthesizers louder and louder until the entire club was pulsating.

I'd been mesmerized. This freaky electronic music was scary and full of rage, yet also romantic—and classic somehow.

Alan smashed the microphone into his face a few times and slammed it to the floor. Martin cut the synths. There was a moment of stunned silence, then screams and applause as the crowd went crazy.

Backstage, Alan had collapsed on a bench in our dressing room, sweating and panting like he'd fought a heavyweight brawl. He didn't say a word, just lit a cigarette and nodded slowly at us kids.

"What about Alan Vega for 'Frankie'?" I asked Ric.

"Oh, he's my friend, he'll come in for sure," Ric said.

When Alan arrived, looking so cool in his dark sunglasses, he asked me, "What's this song about?"

"A friend of mine and his cross-dressing," I said. "Being free to be yourself."

"Cool," Alan mumbled. He lit a cigarette.

"Fuck it up as much as you want," I said.

Alan got on the mic and improvised amazing stuff. His deep voice added the touch of menace and romance that "Frankie" needed.

Now that I had a little money, I wanted to open a club "by the kids, for the kids," where everyone would feel welcome. Boy Bar was closing, so I rented both floors from Paul McGregor, and partnered up with Dean Richards and Kitty Kowalski. I named our club Coney Island High because I loved Coney Island, and the building reminded me of *Rock 'n' Roll High School*. Sure, people might think it was in Brooklyn, but Max's Kansas City wasn't in Kansas City—so what the hell.

This probably wasn't the smartest investment, but I've found over the years that the things I do from the heart always wind up being the most rewarding.

I hired my friends, some old hardcore guys, and a couple Hells Angels. Howie was our DJ, ambassador, and troublemaker. We threw wild drunken dance nights, and lots of great shows from No Doubt and Alex Chilton to Modest Mouse and the Beastie Boys.

It was a fantastic time, except that everyone I hired—

other than the Hells Angels—gave away the bar and let their friends in for free whenever Howie and I were on tour. Howie just rolled his big eyes at me and said, "What did you expect?"

Paul McGregor got a kick out of all the kids in their rock-and-roll threads. We needed this place, and he understood that. But if we were late with the rent, he would zip in on his roller skates, shouting over the music: "I like you guys! I like you guys a lot! But you gotta pay the rent. You gotta pay it on time!"

Meanwhile, the new mayor, Rudy Giuliani, started enforcing petty laws the city had ignored for decades. Cops were arresting people for jaywalking (which is practically a New York art form) or brown-bagging a beer. The city was becoming a police state. Giuliani harassed nightclubs by reinstating a racist old "cabaret law" that banned more than three people from dancing in a bar. It had been passed back in the 1920s to shut down Black jazz clubs. Giuliani's "quality of life" task force raided the downtown clubs nightly. If they even thought they saw anyone dancing, they would turn on all the lights, cut the music, and throw everyone out.

Paul put up with lots of late rent while my partners and I paid lawyers to fight tens of thousands of dollars in fines. If you didn't pay up, the city could padlock your doors. We posted NO DANCING signs all over Coney Island High. People thought we were joking. "What is this, *Footloose?*"

We installed a panic button for our doorman to push the moment the cops arrived. It instantly switched the music inside to classical or something equally undanceable, like Lou Reed's *Metal Machine Music*. Dancers froze like drunken zombies, bewildered. The police would walk in on that bizarre scene, and we'd beat the fine. At least for that night.

Chapter 25

The Hasselhoff

*She had a spark
Like Joan of Arc
—"In the Summer"*

"You guys got the KISS reunion tour!" James Diener told us.

James was D Generation's A&R guy at Columbia Records. He had taken us out to a nice Italian restaurant to surprise us with the big news. KISS was putting the makeup back on, James added, "just like in '78." I flashed back to my fifth-grade teacher, Mr. Liss, so annoyed by my squirrely behavior and KISS obsession that he shouted, "You wanna get to sixth grade, Malin? Let KISS promote you, not Liss!"

I would have given my left nut back then to open for KISS. But now I was too cool for school. Did we really want to open for them in 1996? Howie, Michael, Rick, Danny, and I exchanged doubtful glances over our plates of pasta. Then James handed out the itinerary. One venue popped out: Madison Square Garden. We looked at each other and grinned. We were in.

I couldn't wait to tell my father. I used to invite him to come see me play. His answer was always the same: "I'll see ya when ya play the Garden."

"But Dad, the band is selling out CBGB—three nights in a row."

"Yeah, yeah, get a real job. Cut your hair. The post office is hiring. I'll see ya when ya play the Garden."

"Dad," I came back with a few years later, "we're selling out Irving Plaza."

"Yeah, sure, I'll see ya when ya play the Garden."

D Generation went on tour with KISS in mid-July. The guys in KISS were very welcoming, which we appreciated. Gene Simmons would come by our tiny dressing room and show off his circus tricks, balancing a drumstick or a broom on his nose. Peter Criss's daughter was a D Generation fan, so he brought her to meet us. Paul Stanley stopped in regularly to say hello.

We never saw Ace Frehley, though. We heard Ace had signed a contract saying that if drank any alcohol, he wouldn't get paid. He wisely avoided us. KISS's crew, on the other hand, lived to break our balls. Tony the tour manager was a big, tough, bald Black man. Handing us our laminates, he boomed, "You lose this, you gotta pay $350. And you gotta wear the Hasselhoff for the rest of the tour!" The Hasselhoff was a laminate with *Baywatch* star David Hasselhoff's photo.

The first night, Tony ordered us to stay put in our dressing room during KISS's lengthy sound check. "Can't have any photos getting out!" he barked. Bored, we started tossing ham slices from the deli tray against the walls. Tony barged in and nearly threw us off the tour for "trashing the dressing room like a bunch of assholes." We were tempted to show him how D Generation really trashed a dressing room. But we apologized and swore to behave.

That night, we opened for KISS at Gund Arena in Cleveland. I had no idea how to command a stage that huge. I zoomed around like a nut as we ripped nonstop through our set, playing every song too fast because we were so hyped up. The crowd started yelling: "Bruuuuuuce! Bruuuuuuce!"

Springsteen? I wondered. Was he waiting in the wings to make a guest appearance? Nope. The crowd was simply booing us.

What worked for D Generation when we headlined nightclubs did not impress twenty thousand KISS fanatics in an arena. The audience was mostly middle-aged men who probably hadn't left the house since 1978. "Holy shit, KISS is coming to town. I gotta hit the Walmart and get me some pants!"

D Generation was nothing but the obstacle between them and their heroes. But I wasn't going down without a fight. We tweaked our set every night until we figured out how to win over those die-hard KISS fans. In an arena, sound takes longer to travel. You have to play slower. Keep the backbeat strong and the hooks clear, so people can *feel* your songs.

Danny and I roamed the arena after we played, searching for the few attractive women we could find and inviting them backstage. I'd grown up feeling ugly and rejected. Now, when a good-looking woman was eager to be with me on tour, I couldn't turn her down. That would be like finding a hundred-dollar bill on the floor and not picking it up. I was afraid if I didn't grab it, I'd never see it again. And it can be exciting to meet someone new, and wonder, *What will she be like? Can I make her feel good? Can we do this dance?*

When it's hot, raw, and thrilling, sex can be very life-affirming. Especially after you were just booed onstage. But trying to screw a different person every night can lead you down some dark and lonely paths. It can suck your soul sometimes, leaving you feeling pretty damn empty.

Gene Simmons was a notorious ladies' man. He kept a roadie standing next to the stage during KISS shows for one purpose. If Gene spotted a hot woman while he was playing, he signaled the guy to get her a backstage pass. Unbeknownst to me and Danny, Gene was getting pissed off because we usually got to her first.

Near the end of the tour, KISS gave us a bass drum head signed by each member:

Love you guys! —Paul Stanley

Never forget your true love, rock and roll. —Ace Frehley

Keep on banging! —Peter Criss

D Generation, never ever cock block me again.
—Gene Simmons

As we approached the Madison Square Garden date, the excitement started to tick in my head. So did the memories. My mother taking me and Juliet to the circus when we were kids, and Juliet puking up cotton candy in the car. My first-ever concert: KISS at the Garden when I was ten, sitting way up high in the nosebleed seats, smelling skunky weed.

When Heart Attack broke up, I went to the Garden alone to see Billy Joel. Up in the bleachers again, I told myself, *I'm gonna play here someday.* I'm sure countless kids with rock-and-roll dreams have sat in the cheap seats whispering the very same thing.

We got D Generation's family members great seats in the Garden. I got tickets for old friends like Steve Poss and Jimmy G., too. People came out of the woodwork asking for tickets. How many punks does it take to screw in a light bulb? One to screw it in, and fifty on the guest list.

Remember my summer-camp crush, Lucy Pollard? A few

years after she dumped me, Lucy came around Whitestone, wanting to reconnect. It was like a beautiful dream. She'd come over after school, and we'd drink warm beer and fool around while my mother was at work. I was overjoyed. But another girl liked me, and I got greedy and started seeing her, too. Lucy found out and cut me off cold.

When I started dating Lisa and truly fell in love for the first time, something broke inside me. I felt overwhelmed with guilt for cheating on Lucy. I couldn't sleep or eat for weeks. I had to apologize to her. I reached out but she wouldn't call me back. Lisa even called her for me. Nothing.

Before the Garden show, I stopped by Coney Island High to check my messages. Lucy had called, asking for tickets. I didn't call her back, and I still feel bad about it. I was also juggling a couple of girlfriends at the time.

My relationship with Jenny was rocky, even though I loved her deeply. Jenny played drums in Star Kisst. She had a slender figure, full lips, beautiful green eyes, long brown hair, and a tiny star tattoo on her left cheekbone. She lived in blue jeans slung low across her hips, and had this natural country vibe. The first time I saw her, she got in my van with the band Vacant Lot. She reminded me of Lauren Bacall. Soft, delicate, and pretty, yet there was a toughness and a swagger in the way Jenny moved, and how she smoked her cigarette.

I hung out with her one night at a friend's birthday party downtown, and took her back to my ejector mattress in Greenpoint. The flimsy French doors between my bedroom and Carco's didn't block much noise. It was a little awkward having a date over if Carco was home. And Carco was home most nights now. He had quit drinking—after nearly getting himself killed. Sober, Carco was the sweetest guy. But an unhappiness had been building inside him. He became an angry, troublemaking drunk.

We were at Stromboli Pizza one night scarfing down slices to mop up the booze we'd drunk at the Ritz. Some kid handed us a flier. "No, dick!" Carco yelled. He grabbed the kid's fliers and threw them onto the filthy floor. Punches flew.

Another night, we were drinking at King Tut's Wah Wah Hut. "Can I bum a cigarette?" a guy asked Carco.

"No, dick!" Carco yelled, shoving the guy. A fight broke out again. I'd have to back Carco up, even when I knew we were in the wrong.

One night, we were walking up Clinton Street on the Lower East Side after leaving a party. Carco was drunk and wanted cigarettes, so we wandered into a bodega with salsa blasting from tinny speakers. There was a green metal dumpster in front of it. As we left, Carco pushed the dumpster off its wheels and slammed it to the sidewalk. Two Puerto Rican men charged out of the shop. One pointed a gun at us without saying a word. I saw a second gun in the holster around his hips. I threw up my hands, yelling, "We're really sorry! So sorry!" I quickly lifted the dumpster and rolled it back in place. The guy shoved the gun into his holster and walked back inside. "What the fuck, Stiff?" I screamed at Carco. "You coulda got us killed!"

A few weeks later, Carco and Victor left Continental after a long night of drinking. They lurched along St. Marks Place toward Avenue A. A tough local gang always hung out on the corner near Tompkins Square Park. These crazy motherfuckers carried box cutters, because they got you less jail time than knives. As Victor and Carco approached their corner, Carco tossed an empty bottle up in the air. It crashed to the sidewalk, sending glass flying at the crew. Like a pack of wolves, they quickly surrounded him. Carco was wearing a thick wool overcoat. They sliced it down the back, failing to hit skin. Then someone went for the jugular and slit Carco's throat open right under his jaw. Blood gushed over Carco as he and Victor raced to King Tut's with those guys hot on their backs. Luckily, my old friend Stan was working the door that night. He shoved Carco into the bathroom, grabbed a wad of paper towels, and yelled at Victor to press it against the wound. Stan ran back out and blocked the gang from entering the bar. He snuck Victor and Carco out the side. Victor hailed a cab and rushed Carco to the emergency room. Carco was stitched up just in time, and didn't bleed to death. That was the last night he ever drank.

Now Carco stayed home smoking weed, working out Travis Bickle–style in front of his bedroom mirror, and crashing early. Eventually, Carco was a sweet guy all the time again, and he got to tour the world playing bass for Dee Dee Ramone.

Since Carco was home, I put on some Marvin Gaye to make things feel a little more private for me and Jenny. I started kissing her, and slapped her ass—just once. She liked that a lot, so I spanked her for a while. It really got us going.

After we had sex, instead of finding an excuse to get Jenny out, I realized, to my surprise, that I wanted her to sleep over. We went to the Sunshine Diner for eggs the next morning, before I drove her home. After that, I wanted to be around Jenny all the time.

That afternoon, Carco strolled out of his room. "What the hell were you listening to last night?" he asked.

"Sorry, Stiff, was it too loud?"

"Nah, but you were, like, snapping along to it," Carco said, sauntering around the living room snapping his fingers like Tony Bennett.

I burst out laughing. "Stiff, that wasn't snapping. Lemme tell ya what happened . . ."

* * *

Jenny brought me little gifts when we started dating. Watermelon Jolly Rancher candies in a paper bag, or any fun thing she knew I liked. When she looked into my eyes, I saw an unconditional love I'd only experienced before with my mother. I felt like I could do anything or be anyone, good or bad, and Jenny would still love me and never leave.

The things she loved about me were simple and sweet, like her gifts. A corny dance I'd do in bed, or my crab walk down the street on a cold night. The goofball stuff she said made her fall in love with me even more. "You think you're so wild," she would whisper in my ear, "but you're really not that wild."

Jenny was a talented singer-songwriter with a beautiful voice. She got a record deal, but shot herself in the foot by not always showing up to meetings or recording sessions. Jenny battled with herself, and dealt with it by hiding in bed. She had a tough time waking up to face the day or go to work. She was like a broken bird, and I was familiar with that.

I was in love, but holding something back, like I had promised myself I would. I didn't think leaving our relationship open would hurt as much as it did, though. I'd walk into a party and see Jenny hanging out with some other musician guy, and it would kill me. But I'd still go on tour and keep picking up those hundred-dollar bills.

I was burning hard to keep my freedom; to have my cake and eat it, too. I had this constant need to prove myself . . . and another woman in New York had caught my eye.

Chapter 26

The Garden

I've been high in the mountains
I've been down there in the Tombs
I've been green with envy
I've been black as the blues
—"Saint Christopher"

Raffaele was a statuesque, raven-haired gothic beauty with pale skin and red lips who dressed in corsets and black leather. She was a few years older than me, tough, and cool, with a tattooed panther running down her left arm that I loved to look at while she tended bar at Lismar Lounge. I could tell by watching her on the job that she was strong and smart. But she never paid any attention to me, and I could barely work up the nerve to even talk to her.

When I opened Coney Island High, I asked her to come work there. I discovered that she was very funny, with a dark sarcastic wit, and far more down-to-earth than she looked. Once I really got to know her, I finally had the guts to ask her out.

We enjoyed being together—but for some reason we didn't click in bed. It felt awkward, so we switched gears and became very good friends. Then one night, after Jenny and I had broken up for the hundredth time, Raffaele and I ended up in bed again. This time everything felt great.

Raff didn't need me to take care of her. She was a mama who fiercely defended her friends and had her shit together. She could be possessive and fiery, and had gone to jail years ago for attacking another girl with a bottle in a rage. Sometimes Raff's anger scared me. But the closer we got, the more I saw the sweet, vulnerable girl from Michigan who had lost her father. When I stayed at her place on 3rd and B, everything was clean and organized, perfectly in the right place. Even when I had the worst hangover on the gloomiest winter day, waking up at Raff's made me feel like life was going to be okay. If she had to go before I got up, she would fold my clothes and leave me breakfast with a little note. I found that so comforting.

I had strong feelings for Jenny *and* Raffaele. I really wanted them both at the Madison Square Garden show. In my mind, the place was so huge that I figured if I put Jenny stage left and Raffaele stage right, they'd never see each other.

D Generation's dressing room at the Garden was roughly the size of a tenement bathroom. Once again, we were admonished to stay put while KISS sound-checked. But then Gene Simmons did something really nice. He invited me to join him while he was being filmed giving a tour of the Garden after sound check.

D Generation's second album had just come out. As Gene and I walked through the Garden together, he said, "Jesse, I hope your record goes to number one." The backstage manager wasn't so nice. D Gen's sound check was cut in half. We were also curtly informed that after our set we would not be allowed back into our dressing room—or backstage at all. "Once you're done, grab your stuff and get out," he snarled.

At least I got my father and Papa Artie backstage to come say hello before we played. Steve Van Zandt from the E Street Band popped his head in our dressing room to wish D Gen good luck. Howie's parents were thrilled when they turned around and saw that they had even better seats than Donald Trump.

Despite several tequila shots, my heart was beating really

fast as I stood in the wings, about to go on. *Do not fall off the stage again*, I told myself sternly. We had played Boston a couple nights before. When I'd clocked Aerosmith guitarist Joe Perry in the audience, I got so amped up trying to impress him with my front-man antics that I tumbled right off the seven-foot stage and knocked my back out.

I glanced at my bandmates. We all looked tough and great in our extra-spiky hair and motorcycle boots . . . except for Rick, the Atomic Elf, who had decided to dress like Don Johnson in *Miami Vice* to fuck with the rest of us. Rick was wearing orange polyester slacks, a Hawaiian print shirt, and bright puffy sneakers. He had dyed his hair silver and slicked it back. We were pretty pissed at him, frankly, but the show must go on.

We walked onstage. Suddenly, the brightest lights in the world were in my face, and beyond that all I could see were black silhouettes. The stage was carpeted, with monitors built into the floor so they wouldn't block the audience's view. I felt like a little kid again, running around in my pajamas at night with the living-room rug soft under my feet. Playing air guitar to thousands of tiny lights glittering outside our window. It was like a dream, and flew by in a flash.

After our set, I found Jenny and gave her a big hug. Then I zipped all the way around to the other side of the arena to see Raffaele. She stood glaring as I approached.

"I saw you with Jenny! What the hell is she doing here?"

Uh oh, I guess this place wasn't as big as I thought.

I'd already seen KISS a dozen times, so I decided I would escape to Coney Island High and start celebrating. I felt exhilarated, yet I also had a strange ache inside—a longing to call someone and share this amazing experience. I couldn't figure it out.

Then it hit me: I wanted to call my mom. She would have loved this night. Yeah, my father was there. He took pictures and seemed proud of me—but it wasn't the same. My mother would have really understood what this night meant.

To this day, I get that same feeling whenever something special happens. Even after all this time, it still hits me like a punch in the gut, when I remember that she is gone and I can't call her. I bring her dreams with me wherever I go, and that helps. Papa Artie brought her blood and spirit to Madison Square Garden, and that helped, too.

I grabbed a Rolling Rock and my buddy Rizzo. We stepped out of the Garden into the New York night. We were still under the pavilion when three cops rolled up on us. "Open container!" one barked, pointing at my beer.

"I just played the Garden!" I shouted, waving my laminate at him. I pointed at the marquee. "That's my band, D Generation. We just opened for KISS!"

"Open container!" he barked again.

"I'm not even on the sidewalk yet," I protested. "I'm a New Yorker. I've waited my whole life for this."

Next thing I knew, I was in handcuffs. The cops crammed me into a van with a bunch of other miscreants headed to the Manhattan Detention Complex on White Street, aka the Tombs. It was the most smelly, claustrophobic place I'd ever been. You're shuffled from one crowded pen to the next, descending farther and farther into the subcellar. I was smashed in with drug dealers, thieves, twitching crackheads, and full-on nutjobs. I was given one collect phone call. I called Raffaele, who refused to accept it. That meant I was stuck in the Tombs until I could see the judge on Monday.

Each foul-smelling pen had one slimy seatless toilet in the middle of the room. I didn't eat the bologna sandwich, go to the bathroom, or sleep for forty-eight hours. My biggest fear was getting lost in the system and sent to Rikers Island. The odds of my skinny ass being raped if that happened were pretty high, given my youth, not to mention my arty dreadlocks and eyeliner.

I wound up in a cell with some dealers who worked Washington Square Park. "When we get out, we're gonna go to Mamoun's Falafel on Macdougal!" I yelled. "I'm buying!" They cheered. I said whatever else I could think of to bond with my fellow prisoners. "You play drums? Awesome. Let's form a band when we get out. Your cousin's a rapper? Sure, I'll pass his demo on to my label."

On Monday, I saw the judge. Case dismissed. I went home and took the best shower of my life. Like Rupert Pupkin says in *The King of Comedy*: "Better to be king for a night than schmuck for a lifetime."

Chapter 27

The Pirate Ship

On a chartless course
And you won't be told
—"Here's the Situation"

When my mom and dad were breaking up and their fights got really bad, my mother would grab me and Juliet and leave in the night for her parents' place. Those midnight drives were scary and sad, but also exciting. It felt like we were running away from things that hurt—and into the unknown.

Sometimes my mother drove us upstate to Aunt Irma's worn-down Catskills bungalow. It was from another era, when people from the boroughs could scrape up enough money to get a little nature for the summer and have some fun.

I loved looking out the window as we drove through the mountains, while John Denver and Carole King sang on the radio. I would slip into this dreamy meditative state, where everything felt safe and made sense. If "The Way We Were" came on the radio, though, I'd have to fight back tears. I didn't want to look weak.

Maybe those childhood road trips are why I fell into this pirate-ship life. I love drifting down a sea of highways, lost in my thoughts and the music in my head. I love the feeling of entering a new town for the first time, wondering who I'll meet and what might happen.

* * *

D Generation's tour with KISS kicked off two years of nonstop touring behind our second album, *No Lunch*. Its title came from a call Grandpa Simon made to me from the Bronx Veterans Home, captured on my answering machine.

"I can't hear you," Grandpa Simon groans. "Talk into the phone. Talk into the phone!"

I ask if Juliet and I can meet him for lunch Friday.

"No lunch! No! No! No!" he shouts.

The entire wacky call is a hidden track on the album. It still gets to me. An old man wanting to connect with his grandchildren—you can hear that in his voice. Yet he's throwing up obstacles. I'm like that, too, sometimes. I want love, but I run from things that might hurt.

At first, D Generation toured in a van, with Jack Flanagan as our road manager. Jack and I were tight again. He had become a seasoned pro, handling everybody from the Beastie Boys to Ronnie Spector. Somehow, Jack also found time to get an NYU business degree. "I put it to great use shopping for hummus and rice cakes for bands," he joked.

I ribbed Jack one time about the Jamaican accent he had while he was in the Mob.

"Yeah," he laughed, "I was in H.R.'s army."

Jack was the perfect tour manager for D Gen. He was a big, good-natured guy who always had a smile on his freckled Irish face. But Jack was also a hard-nosed businessman who never let us get ripped off. Jack drove the van, ran the lights, settled the shows, and fought off any all-American assholes who tried to fuck with us.

We were loudmouthed New Yorkers sporting crazy hair, motorcycle jackets, and funny boots. Danny added a furry leopard-print coat he had stolen from his girlfriend's closet that hung to his knees. We'd hit Cracker Barrel for breakfast or go into Walmart, and people would glare at us with such disgust. If looks could kill, we'd have all been dead. Like Grandpa Simon used to say, "Somebody's liable to pass a remark." I'd stare right back at them and chant, *"They're looking. They're looking."* And they'd quickly turn away.

Jack kept us laughing on long drives when we were exhausted and imploding. He kept us healthy with his "crucial mixture"—a secret elixir that instantly cured hangovers. He broke the promoter's balls if the dressing room didn't have every item in our contract. Truthfully, we weren't selling a lot of tickets in some places. The promoters probably didn't have the money to buy the candy, cigarettes, and liquor we had requested. But some did go all out. If we got a bottle of tequila and a fruit plate, we felt like big stars.

When we flew down to Texas for the first time, Jack was waiting at the arrival gate with a couple bags of popcorn. Just seeing his face put me at ease.

"You guys shouldn't blow all that money flying around," my father once said, although his reasoning was a little dated. "Dion didn't get on that plane," he said—referring to the 1959 crash that killed Buddy Holly—"because the ticket cost as much as his parents' rent up in the Bronx." My father also thought I should dress more like Dion onstage, in a nice sweater. But I was usually shirtless, going commando in skin-tight plaid pants my friend Tony Monster made for me.

In San Antonio, I did a split jump off the drum riser and the crotch seam on those pants burst wide open. Everything was hanging out, but I kept singing. I had no idea that two armed Texas Rangers were posted at the club. We didn't have cops with guns at shows in New York. The Rangers marched over to Jack, who was behind the light board. "Y'all better get your boy dressed or we're taking him in."

Jack ran to the side of the stage, yelling, "Cut the naked shit, Malin, or you're going to jail!" He threw my black trench coat at me so I could cover up.

On the drive to New Orleans that night, I had to pee so bad, but Jack refused to stop the van. We were cruising down a dark two-lane highway surrounded by swampland. Maybe he was afraid I'd be dragged off by an alligator. Everyone else was asleep. My seat window only tilted open an inch and a half. I stood sideways and squeezed my penis through the opening. I let loose, not realizing the wind was blowing my piss through the seat window behind me. It soaked Danny's furry coat, which was lying on the seat. He was really mad when he put it on the next morning. I did not confess to the crime. We all hated that coat, anyway.

We crashed on people's floors and couches, and in their guest rooms and basements. Your hosts were your biggest fans—so excited to have you in their homes. They'd keep you up all night showing you their cats and family photos, playing you their favorite records, and inviting all their chain-smoking, beer-guzzling friends over to meet you. All I wanted was to crawl onto the nearest couch and pass out. But I couldn't bear to be rude to people who loved us. Eventually, we realized it was worth spending a few bucks to get a motel room.

Van tours were rough on body, mind, and soul. Often, I just wanted to go home. But like Captain Willard says in *Apocalypse Now*, "When I was here, I wanted to be there; when I was there, all I could think of was getting back into the jungle."

When Columbia Records gave us a large tour-support budget, we blew it on a big shiny bus. Naturally, we hired our friends to be the road crew. We wanted to take as much of

New York with us as we could, so we brought on Jack and two take-no-shit roadies: Michael Sticca and Joe Bruno.

After we'd met Sticca in LA, we didn't see him again for a few months. Then one night, he showed up at a D Generation gig at Irving Plaza. He hopped onstage and started untangling cables and moving mic stands out of our way as if he'd already been our roadie for years.

Sticca told me that on his drive back home to New York, he had decided to stop smack dab in the middle of the country, which he calculated to be Lawrence, Kansas. "I spent a month in Nowheresville laying low," he said.

I stifled a grin imagining Sticca walking around some wholesome Midwest town, dressed in black and weirding out the citizens. He had been on the road since the mid-seventies—yet he never seemed to age. He carried a big black flashlight the size of a horse's cock that could crack a skull. He drank all day, every day; it didn't even faze him. Sticca was the sarcastic Ed Norton to Jack's Ralph Kramden.

Joe Bruno was a boisterous guy with wide shoulders, long muscular arms, and hands like concrete. He dressed like a homeboy in puffy sneakers, shorts, and cut-off basketball jerseys in bright colors. Joe had gotten his teeth bashed in drunkenly fighting a bunch of cops at Yankee Stadium. Now he had big white choppers. He didn't ask many questions. If anyone messed with us, Joe just started punching.

At the Dragonfly in Hollywood, some jerk was taunting Howie. Joe grabbed the guy and began pounding him with his concrete fist, while loudly keeping up a conversation he was having with somebody else.

D Generation's crew made us feel safe. These guys could cheer us up or call us out, as needed. Jack had known me since I was twelve. He wasn't afraid to tell me when I was full of shit. Sticca loved to break everyone's balls and tell us all we were full of shit.

Everybody in D Gen—except Howie—came from a broken home. Our parents were divorced, dead, or had left. Jack and Sticca were like our parents on the road. Joe was the big brother who had our backs. These guys were funny as hell, too. They clowned around and kept five needy rockers who were at each other's throats half the time from killing each other.

Getting a tour bus made road life more comfortable, but our camaraderie began to fade. We were drifting apart into our own bunks, under our own headphones. We weren't singing along to the same songs in the van anymore, or laughing at the same jokes together.

I loved Howie's energy, but we fought over the stage. He didn't hang back near the drums like a typical bass player. He got right up front, headbanging and running around. When he got in my way, I'd block him with my mic stand and he'd get really pissed off.

Rick was a beautiful songwriter, but his new songs kept getting rejected by the band. Rick reacted by cranking techno in the bus lounge and dressing like a raver. He started disappearing after shows, partying at warehouses all night. Finally, Rick left to form his own band.

Todd Youth came on board as Rick's replacement. I'd known Todd since he was a thirteen-year-old runaway playing in New York hardcore bands. This good-looking stringbean in black jeans and Converse sneakers became an incredible guitarist, working with everyone from Glenn Danzig to Glen Campbell. He really took us up a notch.

D Generation and our crazy crew were New York City on wheels. Social Distortion singer Mike Ness loved that, and brought us on tour for two months.

Social Distortion's audience was a bunch of tattooed, muscular Mike Ness look-alikes in white tank tops and greased-back hair. Boy, did they hate us. They threw chains and bottles, and spit at us. I even got hit in the head with a flying sneaker. We'd get back to the safety of our bus feeling pretty beaten down. But after hanging with our crew, joking and goofing around, we were ready to go out there the next night and piss off more knuckleheads.

In San Francisco, a short kid with black hair and green eyes came up to me while I was watching Social Distortion from the balcony. He was Billie Joe Armstrong from Green Day. To my surprise, he asked me about some D Generation songs. I was shocked that he'd even heard of us. A few months later, Green Day invited us to open for them on an American tour.

On most big tours, the support act is shoved onstage while the venue is still half empty. But Green Day was so cool. They always had us wait until the place was packed. We played to a full house every night. To our surprise, Green Day's audience loved us.

Billie told me later that he had warned his band: "Watch out, these D Gen guys are gonna be pretty wild and fucked up." We laughed, because on tour he found out that we were just a bunch of nerdy music geeks from Queens.

Green Day's show was so tight that I asked Jack to start videotaping our set. Every night on the bus, Howie, Danny, Todd, Michael, and I watched the tape and critiqued our performance. It wasn't fun. We ripped each other apart and got into some nasty fights. But this quickly tightened up our act.

The tour wrapped up with three nights at the Fillmore in San Francisco. At the after-party, the Green Day guys gathered us all together and asked: "Do you wanna go to Europe with us?" This was right before Christmas 1997, and what a great gift it was. I was very excited, but also scared about traveling overseas. Knowing Jack was coming along eased my anxiety a bit.

I roomed with Todd, who had toured Europe a lot. He taught me how to call home, deal with different currencies, and sanitize our hotel rooms with baby wipes and Lysol. To survive on the road, he said, "ya gotta take a lotta cat naps. Grab sleep wherever you can."

European audiences embraced D Generation like only a few US cities ever did. I couldn't believe that the songs we had worked up at Giorgio's were carrying us to such incredible places. There's nothing better than a rowdy audience in Glasgow or Paris singing along at full blast.

I invited photographer Bob Gruen and his wife, Elizabeth, onto the pirate ship for this tour. Even with Bob, I felt awkward posing for photos. Still do. I lean on the same unsmiling expression that I know works. Do I think I look goofy, vulnerable, or just not cool when I smile? Probably all three. Grandpa Simon never smiled in photos either. Then again, he jumped out of a second-story window.

After every show, we hung around the bar or the merch table—meeting fans, signing their records, their T-shirts, their skin. Someone telling us that our music got them through a hard time meant the world to us.

The more I traveled, the more I realized how small this planet is, and how much every human being wants to connect and be loved. We're alive right now, at this time, together. Whatever race, religion, or creed—if you cut us open, we all bleed the same.

Chapter 28

Christmas on Fifth

Got some cigarettes
I don't need anyone
And no real regrets
I don't need anyone
—"Solitaire"

When D Generation toured with the Ramones in 1993, Joey stayed on our bus. The Ramones were in a van. They already knew what we had yet to learn: *Don't waste your money on a stupid tour bus.* The Ramones ate Domino's Pizza every single night on tour.

"Why?" I asked Joey. "You guys could have the best pizza in town. Why are you eating that junk?"

"'Cause it's always the same," he said.

I got that. Everything changes every day on the road. It's nice to have one thing you can count on.

Legroom wasn't the only reason Joey hung out on our bus. He and Johnny Ramone had stopped speaking many years earlier, after Johnny stole his girlfriend, Linda, and eventually married her.

Joey struggled with OCD before most people had ever heard of it. Howie and Johnny used to tiptoe behind Joey on the sidewalk, giggling as he compulsively stepped on and off the curb. Sometimes Joey got stuck locking and unlocking his apartment while the Ramones sat waiting in the van for him. And sometimes Monte had to drive Joey all the way back to the airport to touch certain walls before he would go home.

OCD made Joey a creature of habit, and he folded me into his routine. Every morning at nine, Joey put on his sneakers and leather pants, and went for oatmeal at Veselka. He'd grab a Starbucks Frappuccino on the way home and call me hopped up on sugar and caffeine. I was never awake that early, so Joey would leave a sweet, rambling message on my answering machine.

"Hey Jesse, it's Joey. How ya doin'? I got some great ideas for my birthday show at Coney. I'm really excited. I got Jonathan Richman. Maybe we can get Noddy from Slade, Ronnie Spector, the Independents. And D Gen, of course. It's gonna be great. Call me back. What are ya listening to? I'm listening to Supergrass. They are so great. Okay, Jesse, let's talk. Call me back."

Joey's entire life was music. A lot of rock stars are driven by fame, drugs, sex, or money. Not Joey. He was always about the music. He listened to records and the radio constantly. Joey's ears were wide, and he knew everybody.

When I finally did crawl out of bed, Joey would be my first call. He always asked me the same question: "What are you listening to?"

"I heard this female singer with this raw, beautiful voice on Steve Earle's new album," I once told Joey. "It really hit my heart. Like no one I've ever heard before."

"Lucinda Williams!" he exclaimed. "I know her. I did a songwriting panel with her at the Bottom Line. She's great."

While in Los Angeles, I went to see Lucinda at the Wiltern. Her show changed my life. She had the swagger of Keith Richards, the storytelling magic of Bob Dylan, and the voice of an earthbound, hard-living angel. I bought all her records. I couldn't wait to tell Joey.

I was starting to feel like D Generation had run its course.

We had been together for seven years, having more fun than should be legal. But our image always overshadowed our songs. I was really sick of reading in the press that we were a "glam-rock hair band."

I began spending hours on long tour drives listening to Lucinda, Wilco, Counting Crows, Whiskeytown, Neil Young, and Steve Earle. I felt inspired to stop hiding behind my hair extensions and attention-grabbing stunts. I wanted to be more vulnerable and personal. I wanted to strip away the artifice and let the songs stand on their own. I needed to try something else while I was still hungry. I felt scared, but that was okay. It was just the roller coaster ticking up the track again.

Some of the D Generation guys were ready to call it quits, too. We played our last show at Coney Island High in April 1999.

In June of that same year, Coney was finally closed down—another victim of Mayor Giuliani's "quality of life" campaign. We couldn't pay those huge fines, and our doors were padlocked—for good.

Howie got hired to play bass for ex-Misfits singer Glenn Danzig's band. I was happy for Howie, but when he left for Los Angeles, I cried. For us to no longer be roommates or play in a band together felt like the end of an era—and I was losing a brother. But I knew we'd still talk on the phone. And I would see him when I was in LA.

For four hundred dollars a month, I rented a crooked little apartment with a bathtub in the kitchen on the safest block in New York—thanks to the Hells Angels clubhouse across the street. It was the only block downtown where you didn't need bars on your windows.

I shared new songs I was writing with Joey. He especially

loved "Solitaire." I wrote it for my friend Kelly Keller, a wild Southern spirit. We loved to go out dancing to old soul and R&B.

I visited Kelly after she moved back to New Orleans, and asked her if she was seeing anybody. "I got some cigarettes and no real regrets," Kelly said. "I don't need anyone."

She overdosed on heroin not long after.

With no record deal and Coney Island High going under, I was broke as a spoke. I needed to figure out something.

"I just want a little bar," I told my buddy Johnny T., who played drums in Clowns for Progress. "Like the places that make us feel at home on tour."

Johnny wanted to take over the old A7. It had been King Tut's Wah Wah Hut, then Wally's, and then it caught on fire.

"No way," I said. "It's jinxed, forget it."

"We'll get a rabbi, we'll burn some sage, we'll call some Rastas!" Johnny said. He talked me into opening our bar Niagara on the best corner in the East Village.

Our policy was that any touring band could drink for free, and DJ if they wanted. Word got around that Niagara was a pretty cool hang. Local bands still played in the back sometimes—only now the bass drum had a real skin, instead of a pizza box.

In June, Joey and I went to see Joe Strummer and the Mescaleros at Irving Plaza. It was Strummer's first New York show in ten years and the place was packed. We watched from the balcony as he played his heart out.

"I was talking to my friend Jesse Malin before the show . . ." Joe told the audience, pointing up at me.

What? I hadn't talked to him in months.

". . . and I hear that Jesse's club got closed down—for dancing! What the hell is going on in this town?"

The audience looked up at me and cheered. Later, Bob Gruen explained that he had told Joe about Coney closing. Like a true pro, Strummer worked it up into a stage bit.

After the show, Joe headed to Niagara, with around four hundred people. He hung out until the sun came up taking photos, sharing stories, answering every question.

I noticed Shane MacGowan from the Pogues slouched in the corner, and went over to say hello. "Yarr," Shane growled like a drunken pirate. He smiled at me with his rotten teeth.

I've never seen any artist be more accessible to his fans than Joe. His dressing rooms were jammed, like that scene in the Marx Brothers's movie *A Night at the Opera* when the characters just keep piling in. Joe would come offstage a sweaty mess, rip off his shirt, grab a drink, and dive into the party.

As the Mescaleros tour continued, I got calls from friends: "Joe Strummer's in my car." "Joe's in my kitchen." "We went out all night!" Strummer could walk into any bar, in any town, and get the whole place up singing and dancing until dawn. If you were going out with Joe, you'd better bring your sunglasses. No wonder his home was deep in the English countryside. He needed a quiet place to recharge. Because everywhere he went, he couldn't help but give everything.

My share of Niagara's profits just covered my rent—with little to spare. Joey loaned me five thousand bucks to make a record with my new band, Bellvue. I had Johnny Pisano on bass, Esko Poldvere from Estonia on guitar, and Joe Rizzo on drums. The music was pounding and distorted, but we also took on the more intimate, personal songs I was writing. I was trying to find my way, I guess.

In December 2000, we went into RPM Studios with Daniel Rey. We put in twelve-hour days, cramming as much into each expensive session as possible.

One afternoon while recording, I got an excited call at the studio from Joey: "Hey, Jesse, U2 invited me to *Saturday Night Live* tonight. Can you go with me? They dedicated a song to me at Irving the other night and I missed it. I feel bad. I gotta go."

"Wow, that's so cool!" I said. "But I'm in the studio. I can't leave."

"Ah, okay."

I could tell Joey was disappointed. He called back a little while later: "You sure you can't go, just for a little bit?"

I turned to Daniel and whispered, "I gotta go." I loved Joey too much to let him down. He really didn't have a lot of friends; he kept his circle very small. He was also quietly battling lymphoma. "Time to take my Molotov cocktail," he'd joke about the drugs his doctors prescribed. Like my mother, Joey sought to "hide it from the kids." Only his family and a few close friends knew.

"Okay, Joey," I finally said, "let's go."

If New York casts the shadow for the perfect crime, it's also the setting for a perfect Christmas. During the holidays, I see the city in beautiful black-and-white, sparkling with magic straight out of *Miracle on 34th Street*. Maybe it's the romantic in me. I visit St. Patrick's Cathedral, buy warm chestnuts from corner carts, and go ice-skating like some hot-chocolate-drinking goofball. I love hearing Christmas songs in the shops around town.

It can be lonely, though, depending on where you're at with love and family. I'm prone to the holiday blues, and often work straight through to avoid feeling down. But I do love the peaceful silence that falls over the city on Christmas Day.

As Joey and I walked through Rockefeller Center on our way to *SNL*, people yelled, "Hey, Joey!" They were so excited to see him. The world just opened up to us. We stopped to gaze up at the big tree, ablaze with lights and shining ornaments. This was nice, enjoying a bit of the spirit with my friend.

I told Joey about the time I wound up on *Saturday Night Live* on Halloween when I was fourteen. Fear was the musical guest that night—and word spread like wildfire through the DC and New York hardcore scenes that if we showed up, we'd be able to get into the studio. John Belushi had hooked this up. He was a huge hardcore fan who loved to go crazy in the pit. Fear was his favorite band.

That's how a bunch of us wound up slam-dancing on national television on October 31, 1981, while Fear tore it up. I dove off the stage straight at the cameras a bunch in my leather jacket with *MASSACRE* painted on the back.

"This is all Belushi's fault!" some lady screamed as a camera tipped over and crashed to the floor.

Ian MacKaye from Minor Threat grabbed a mic and yelled, "New York sucks!" Some DC kid stomped onstage holding a giant pumpkin over his head, then smashed it to the ground. A big chunk went flying and clocked *SNL*'s stage manager.

The show went to dead air as a pumpkin fight broke out onstage and spilled into the audience. Cops rushed in wielding nightsticks and chased us out. Fear was banned from *SNL*, and Belushi died four months later at the Chateau Marmont in Los Angeles.

The next day, the *New York Post* screamed: "FEAR RIOT LEAVES 'SATURDAY NIGHT' GLAD TO BE ALIVE!" The article blamed "slam-banging—a new punk craze that involves dancing, biting, and kicking," and reported that we'd caused more $200,000 in damages to the studio. In truth, it was more like $20,000.

When I went back to school on Monday, my science teacher, Mr. Schlackman, growled, "I know where *you* were this weekend. I saw you jumping off that stage. Wasn't that past your bedtime?" He was breaking my balls, but I could tell he had gotten a kick out of seeing me on TV. I pictured good old Schlackman drinking a beer in his recliner. Suddenly, one of his students pops up on *SNL*, zooming around like a maniac. Probably made his night.

When Joey and I reached 30 Rock, we were whisked into U2's dressing room on the eighth floor. They were lovely guys, incredibly respectful to Joey.

Bono cracked open some beers for us, and pointed to his throat. "My voice is blown," he croaked.

"Go in the bathroom and turn on all the hot water faucets," I said. "Breathe in as much steam as you can."

"Good idea," Bono rasped, and zipped out the door.

Joey and I were escorted to seats right on the edge of the soundstage. Cameras on cranes floated over our heads.

When U2 started playing "Beautiful Day," Joey tried to push me onto the stage. "C'mon, Jesse, get up there. Dive off the stage."

"No way," I said. "Shhh, cut it out, you're the guest of honor."

But Joey's rascally sense of humor had kicked in. He gave me another shove. "Ah, c'mon, man, go for it. Get up there."

It was tempting, I have to admit. But I managed to restrain myself.

After the show, Bono, Joey, and I walked down Fifth Avenue together to the after-party. Joey answered all of Bono's questions about the Ramones in his thoughtful, humble way. I felt happy and at peace.

Bono was mobbed as soon as we entered the ritzy party.

Joey and I found a corner table and sat down. I was tired, and I could tell by the slow way Joey was moving that he was exhausted, too. We didn't get any drinks; we were happy to just relax and check out the shenanigans.

SNL producer Lorne Michaels was going table to table. He reached us in his sharp suit and said, "Hey, Joey!" with a big smile.

Joey shot him a disgusted look. This clearly perplexed Lorne, who was no doubt used to the entire world kissing his ass. "How come you never asked us to be on *SNL*?" Joey demanded, looking Lorne straight in the eye. "New York and the Ramones are synonymous."

"I think we *did*," Lorne replied cheerily.

"Nah," Joey shrugged, "we never got a call."

I stifled a laugh as Lorne began frantically waving at some star across the room. He couldn't get away from us fast enough.

When I dropped Joey off, he asked, like he always did, "You wanna come up and watch a movie or something?" He never liked to go home alone.

Sometimes I said, "Sure." But that night I was too drained, so I begged off.

Four months later, Joey was gone. He died on Easter Sunday, as his brother Mickey played him "In a Little While" by U2.

I wish I had said yes more often.

Chapter 29

O Sole Mio

*And even though the world was blue
We did the best that we could do*
—"Keep On Burning"

I was standing outside Niagara one warm spring afternoon in 2000 when a pale young guy with a Shockabilly haircut approached me. He was dressed in black from his studded denim jacket to his Frankenstein monster boots. Despite his tough exterior, there was a softness about him.

"Are you Jesse?" he asked with a charming smile.

I nodded.

"I'm Tony. I just got here from Denver. Joe Strummer told me to come see you about a job. I'll barback, clean the place. I'll do anything!"

How could I refuse? I gave the kid a shot.

Tony was a great barback, and quickly became our best bartender. He was smart, organized, and hardworking. So I made him Bellvue's road manager, too, for our upcoming cross-country tour.

We borrowed a weird old van from Kitty Kowalski outfitted with a driver's seat, a passenger seat, and a bolted-down wooden bench in the back. This wasn't going to be the most comfortable ride across the country, but the price was right. Tony drove like a champ on the road, sipping on an ever-present bottle of ginseng. He was passionate about packing the van just right—and he made the best mixtapes.

I woke up in El Paso to Marty Robbins singing "El Paso" on the van boom box. Pulling into Nevada, it was "Viva Las Vegas." Tony had mapped out our entire tour, song by song. We called him Tony Rock'n'Rolla. I was really happy Joe had sent this great guy my way.

We planned to stop in Denver for a July 4 barbecue at a friend's house. But first, Tony wanted to make a detour to Missoula, Montana. He was obsessed with getting brass knuckles. Missoula was the brass-knuckle capital of the USA, like Times Square was for switchblades, I guess. Twenty-one states had outlawed brass knuckles, but not good old Montana. Back then, you had to travel for your weapons. So, on we drove to Missoula, with me on the bench shouting, "Mizzula, Mizzula!" turning it into some kinda Jewish thing.

Tony went shopping. The rest of us killed time eating veggie burgers in a hipster coffee shop, listening to Tom Waits on the jukebox. Tony got his knuckles, and we headed to Denver.

The Bellvue tour was fun, but we weren't really finding an audience. Our sound careened all over the place, from noisy rockers to my new rootsy stuff. I was still trying to figure it all out.

I heard that Whiskeytown singer Ryan Adams used to torment his bandmates by blasting D Generation in their van on tour. We met when he came to see D Gen play in North Carolina, and stayed in touch. Now Ryan was having good success with his first solo album, *Heartbreaker*. He encouraged me to go solo, too. "You write the songs, you book the gigs," he said. "You pay for everything. Just do it."

I dismissed that idea; it seemed so adult. I'd have to sit on a stool, pick an acoustic guitar, and wear Hush Puppies.

I was lying on the sand on Jones Beach with my friend Tara one day, and all my anxieties came tumbling out. "I don't know what to do next. I'm so confused."

"You're just scared to be Jesse Malin," Tara responded.

Right then and there I realized, yeah, I was fucking scared. "You're right," I said.

If somebody dares me to do something—whether it's surfing on top of a subway train or going onstage without a band—I have to do it. Something Daniel Glass said once stuck with me: Life is about showing up. Even when you want to hide, force yourself to show up. Something might happen that could change your life.

I booked a Wednesday-night residency at a little club on Avenue A called Brownies. I asked Joe McGinty, who lived around the corner, to accompany me on keys. I called it the "So Low Show."

I felt awkward and exposed without a loud band to drive me forward and get me out of my head. I hated the silence when I tuned my guitar, so I began telling stories between songs. I worked on these bits until I was getting some laughs.

I started recording demos at Pilot Studios on 9th Street. Merle Chinook snuck me in late at night when the studio wasn't booked, in exchange for free drinks at Niagara. On September 10, 2001, I was there late working on my song "High Lonesome." Finally the producer, Bryce Goggin, said, "Okay, Jesse, we've got to wrap it up. The only time I can get you in again is tomorrow morning at nine thirty." I grumbled, because I never, ever got up before one in the afternoon. But I was hell-bent on finishing these songs.

I dragged my ass out of bed the next morning at the ungodly hour of eight thirty. As I was leaving around nine, I ran into my long-haired, metalhead neighbor in the hallway. "You gonna go put out the fire?" he said, flashing me the devil horns with both hands. I had no idea what he was talking about. I stepped outside and headed west on Third

Street. It was one of those crystal-clear days New York gets in September. The sky was the most beautiful bright blue.

As I reached First Avenue, I saw people standing stock-still on the sidewalk, staring downtown. Even weirder, some people were standing on top of cars. So I climbed up onto a parked car and then onto a van. I saw thick black smoke pouring out of the World Trade Center's North Tower, and flames in the sky. Suddenly, a silver jet flew straight into the South Tower. I couldn't believe my eyes. People were screaming.

Steve Poss's mother, Rosalie, worked on the forty-fourth floor of the South Tower. She told Poss that when the first plane hit the North Tower, an announcement blared over her office intercom: *"There is no need to evacuate. The building is safe and secure. For your safety, please remain at your desks."* Mrs. Poss muttered, "Fuck that," and left her coffee and cruller on her desk. She walked down forty-four flights of stairs, and felt the shock in the stairwell when the second plane hit the South Tower. She made it out and walked over the Brooklyn Bridge all the way home to Rego Park, Queens.

D Generation's drummer Michael was released from detox that morning. He emerged from the subway at West 4th Street—freshly clean and sober—into New York City's worst nightmare.

I was in shock. I didn't know what to do, so I just kept walking to Pilot Studios. The city became eerily quiet, save for the distant sound of sirens. When I got to Pilot, Bryce was in the lounge crying, watching the news on the TV. I gave him a hug before I left. I had to find Raffaele and make sure she was safe. I headed down Fifth Avenue to Patricia Field, the 8th Street boutique where Raff worked.

When I reached the store, Pat Field was standing out front with her blazing red hair, smoking a cigarette. "Raff isn't here," she said. We stood silently on the empty sidewalk for a few minutes. Then I felt compelled to walk to Niagara.

When I arrived, I pulled up the metal gates, went inside, and turned on every television in the bar. People from the neighborhood started flooding in. I had never tended bar before, but I immediately began pouring beers and shots, giving them away. Soon, Niagara was packed with friends and neighbors. We were all freaked out and didn't know what to do. The televisions were full of horror.

When the South Tower collapsed, the cell phone stations on its roof were destroyed. Nobody's cell phone was working. I used Niagara's landline, in between serving drinks, to call my sister and friends to make sure they were safe. I reached Raff at her place and she was okay. I reached Vinny at the Vespole house in Brooklyn; he told me everyone was accounted for except Skel, who had gone to work that morning at Dow Jones & Co. They were desperate to reach him, but the office phones were dead.

Skel, who had recently gotten sober for the first time in his life, led the evacuation of the Dow Jones office. He herded up frightened executives, and convinced stubborn reporters to evacuate who were refusing to leave their desks because the biggest story in the world was breaking. Skel evacuated more than a hundred people as waves of debris roared across the streets like a concrete tsunami.

Covered in white dust, Skel made his way to the Hudson River. He was whisked on a barge to triage tents that had been hastily set up in Jersey City. From there, he was taken to a cop's house, so that he could shower and try to contact his family.

When Skel arrived, the cop was pounding cans of beer from a six-pack to calm his nerves. He held a can out to Skel and asked, "You drink?" Skel turned around and left.

He walked for hours with a stranger who was finally able to reach his wife on his cell phone. She picked them up on the side of some New Jersey highway.

For a guy who had been a drunken mess on the job for twenty-five years, Skel was a star on 9/11. He received a medal and a hefty sum from the city for saving all those people.

Paul "Skel" Vespole died of lung cancer in May 2005, a New York City hero. He received a military funeral. As a soldier played taps, Tony Vespole was handed the American flag which had covered Paul's coffin, folded thirteen times into a triangle.

Paulie will forever live in my heart, and in my songs.

Chapter 30

The Crown

From the eve of destruction
To the valley of tears
—"Aftermath"

The day after 9/11, a sickening smell began to reach my neighborhood—a hot mix of scorched metal and burnt flesh. People were walking around in gas masks.

Carco, Rizzo, and I decided to get out of the East Village and go for a jog around Central Park. When we got uptown, the air smelled fine. People were going about their day, almost as if nothing had happened. Rizzo and I finished the six-mile run; Carco quit after the first mile. He didn't drink anymore, but the kid still smoked like a fiend.

Downtown, the following weeks were sad and horrible. Every lamppost, fence, and wall in Union Square Park was covered with homemade fliers and photos of the missing. Friends who had been inside or near the World Trade Center told me their horror stories. Blood and water gushing down the stairs as they evacuated the towers. People leaping out of windows to escape the flames. Airplane passengers falling from the sky, still belted into their seats. My city had been attacked. I was shocked and stunned. But I had grown up with headlines telling New York to "drop dead." I figured we were on our own again.

Three weeks later, I headed out on a cross-country tour in a minivan, with Johnny Pisano on bass and an eager new keyboard player. We were playing the songs I had written during my Brownies residency, and planned to pick up drummers along the way.

To save money, Johnny and I crashed with friends. After a good show in Chicago, we parked in front of Erin Smolinski's house. The next morning, we stepped outside and our van was gone. I rubbed my tired eyes. Still gone.

"Shit, the cops must've towed it," Erin said. "The marathon is today." She drove us to the police station. They sent us to a tow lot. We searched for hours. No van. We went back to the precinct and reported it stolen.

Eight hours later, the police called to tell us the van was in a different lot. We grabbed it, and stopped by the precinct to take it off the "hot sheet." Johnny and I split right away, praying we could still make our next gig in Denver.

As I drove us through Dixon, Illinois, I made a face at the billboard celebrating its native son, Ronald Reagan. Outside of town, on a dark two-lane stretch, police lights flashed in my rearview mirror and I pulled over. The patrol car parked behind us, but the cops didn't get out.

"Holy shit," I said to Johnny, "I think they're calling for backup."

A second police car zoomed up. Four officers jumped out and surrounded our minivan. They hauled Johnny and me out, shoved us onto our knees on the blacktop, and put guns to our heads. I was shaking as I held up my hands, and not just from the cold.

Apparently, our van was still on the hot sheet; these cops thought we'd stolen it. I tried to explain, but they handcuffed us and threw us into the backseat of the squad car. A German shepherd stuck its nose through the metal mesh behind our heads, barking like it couldn't wait to rip us to shreds.

One cop examined my driver's license. "You from New York?"

"Yes sir."

"Near where it happened?"

"Yeah, I live about two miles from where it happened."

Suddenly, everything changed. These officers flipped from ice-cold bastards to the nicest, most sympathetic guys. Even the dog stopped growling. "I believe you boys," he said. "You can go."

Johnny and I experienced incredible hospitality and kindness on that tour. People expressed such love and compassion for the terror New York had experienced. For that rare moment in time, it felt like we were all connected as Americans.

When I got home, though, some slumlord had bought my building. He was paying off rent-controlled tenants so he could jack up the rents on the safest block in New York. "I'll give you twenty thousand to get the hell out," he said when he came to my door. I took the money—thinking maybe I could make an album with it—and moved farther down the Lower East Side to a little apartment on Rivington Street. I used five thousand dollars to pay off my debts, so I could walk along some other blocks and be safe.

"Ya need a ballad," my father would nag me when I was in D Generation. "What's Queen's biggest hit?"

"'Bohemian Rhapsody,'" I would groan.

"What's Zeppelin's biggest hit?"

"I know," I'd say, rolling my eyes, "'Stairway to Heaven.'"

"A ballad, right. What about your boys KISS? What's their biggest hit? 'Beth'!"

"I know, Dad, I knooow."

I never really wrote a ballad for D Generation. But now I was writing lots of them. I found comfort writing in public places—cafés, diners, bars. I liked to walk around grabbing lines from things I'd hear people say. I'd come home with a pocket full of notes scrawled on cocktail napkins. Composition notebooks and cassette tapes were strewn across my kitchen table, along with my faithful companion, a Sony Walkman knockoff, which I took everywhere. I taped song ideas in dressing rooms, bathrooms, and even at the gym. If I heard a melody on the treadmill, I'd hit *Record* and sing over my pounding feet.

Writing for myself—and not a band—was liberating. I dove into my childhood in songs like "Almost Grown" and "Riding on the Subway." Messing up my relationship with Jenny inspired "Brooklyn" and "Wendy." I started to face my taste for the crash-and-burn.

Wendy left me all alone
No postcard or telephone
Wintertime down by the beach
In a jukebox bar way out of reach

"X-mas" was for Raffaele. I gave it to her on a cassette tape for Christmas after we broke up, hoping she'd give me another chance.

Christmas is coming down
Ten-dollar bill in my pocket
I let my baby down
I want to blast off like a rocket

Sonny in *Dog Day Afternoon*, McMurphy in *One Flew Over the Cuckoo's Nest*, Travis Bickle in *Taxi Driver*—these guys do bad things but have big hearts and good intentions. They're motivated by love, even if it's misguided or warped.

There's always a moment when they could stop the madness and try to save themselves. But they can't help but go down with the ship.

I understood that reckless rush. I had that tendency to wreck things before they wrecked me. Maybe I didn't believe I deserved a home—or a love—that would last. They say tragedy + time = comedy. Sometimes it equals a song.

I was floundering that winter. I'd been in bands most of my life. I wasn't sure who I was without one. Like New York, I had a hole in my soul. The holidays were somber in the city, too. No one felt like celebrating after what had happened. Things were bleak. But my buddy Dennis Borowsky, aka Radio Rahim, had an idea . . .

Dennis was a skinny music enthusiast from Long Island with tons of energy. He interviewed me on his KROC radio show when I was in D Generation, and we hit it off right away. I loved bumming around with Dennis in his car, cracking jokes and blasting the radio. He had a spiritual side, and I was drawn to that, too. His big idea was that on New Year's Day we should go to the ocean and release all the bad stuff that had gone down in 2001.

We drove out to Coney Island that afternoon, and walked through the deserted amusement park. The place was desolate. Some nut could have hacked us to pieces on the boardwalk while we screamed bloody murder and no one would have heard us.

On the streets, all that was left from a recent snowstorm was dirty gray slush. But to our surprise, the beach was covered with pristine white snow. Dennis and I dashed across it like little kids, racing to the water hooting and hollering. One of Dennis's sneakers flew right off his foot, but he didn't even stop.

We stood shivering at the edge of the Atlantic, me in soaked sneakers and Dennis in one wet sneaker and one wet sock. We sucked in chestfuls of cold salty air, and gave the ocean all our pain and sorrow. Then we closed our eyes and quietly sent our hopes and dreams for the new year into the universe.

We hiked back to the boardwalk, searching fruitlessly for Dennis's shoe. We were laughing hysterically trying to find that white sneaker, lost in the white snow.

When we got to the car, Dennis cranked up the heat and drove back to Manhattan. I felt clean, fresh . . . purified. Something inside me had shifted. And that year, things did change for the better.

Diane Gentile was a good-looking tough cookie, the daughter of a Queens cop. She was also a talented singer-songwriter and a music executive who worked with artists like Warren Zevon. I trusted Diane's ear and sent her my demos. Diane thought I had enough good songs to make an album and became my new manager.

"I'll be your producer!" Ryan Adams declared.

"I can't afford you," I grinned.

"I'll do it for free."

Diane booked six days at Loho Studios, and I bought a few reels of two-inch tape. We were making this record old-school. I had Johnny on bass and McGinty on keys, plus drummer Paul Garisto, who had a swing to his playing like nobody else. Ryan was going to cover lead guitar.

We recorded everything live, including my vocals. In just six days, *The Fine Art of Self-Destruction* was done.

I eagerly played it for Giorgio. "This is horrible, Jesse!" he cried. "The singing is terrible. You need to recut your vocals." But I loved the lo-fi sound and loose live feel we had captured. This record felt honest to me, with all its imperfections.

Unfortunately, I couldn't score a record deal in the US of A.

"Ever think of wearing a cowboy hat and moving to Nashville?" my father said. "Ya kinda got a country thing going on here."

"Dad," I countered, "I'm gonna be who I am."

Diane never took no for an answer. She flew to England and banged on record company doors. She got me a deal with One Little Indian, an indie label run by Derek Birkett. He had been in anarchist punk bands and managed Björk. This sounded good to me.

The Fine Art of Self-Destruction came out overseas that November. To everyone's surprise—especially mine—it got rave reviews, including "album of the month" in British magazines like *Uncut* and *Mojo*. The London *Times* gave it five stars. I ran to Gem Spa on Second Avenue every week to buy all the imported music magazines and search for more reviews. When I read them, I felt understood—maybe for the first time.

The label flew me and Diane to London for some promo. We stayed at the Columbia, a seedy Victorian-era hotel near Hyde Park. The concierge was a cranky old guy who looked like a butcher and tended bar out of a little cupboard. You had to beg him to open it up, and quickly grab a drink before he slammed it shut again. One day, the Columbia might be jammed with rock bands and hangers-on, like a scene out of *Spinal Tap*. The next day, it could be deserted and creepy, like the hotel in *The Shining*. I wandered into the basement once and couldn't find my way out. I was spooked for days.

I loved London. Every street reminded me of a song: "Waterloo Sunset," "Carnaby Street," the Leicester Square kid in "Russian Roulette." I was thrilled when I spotted the Crown bar. *Wow, that's in the Clash song "Stay Free"!* Turns out there were as many bars named the Crown in London as there were Ray's Pizzas in New York.

I loved drinking a Guinness in those old pubs and listening to people talk. You could feel centuries of history . . . and smell it, too, seeping through the walls like the ghost of Charles Dickens's piss.

In Amsterdam, I did two long days of back-to-back phone interviews at Hotel Prins Hendrik, in the room where Chet Baker had fallen out the window and died. It was only on the second floor; he must have had too many sodas. Downstairs, the front desk was getting fed up. "That fucking Jew with all his phone calls," Diane heard the receptionist sneer.

When I got home, Ryan invited me to open his six-week European tour. "You can't bring McGinty," he said. "It's got to be a fair fight. I'm playing solo and so are you."

My father was going into the hospital for heart surgery. "Whatever happens to me," he said, "you don't stop. You stay on this tour." I could tell he finally believed in what I was doing.

The night before my flight to London, Joe Strummer came into town. I called Diane, Johnny Pisano, and Ryan. "Strummer's here. You gotta come meet him!"

We met up with Joe, Bob and Elizabeth Gruen, and photographer Josh Cheuse at the Cedar Tavern, a famous old hangout for painters and Beat poets back in the fifties.

I asked Joe about his beautiful wife: "How's Luce doing?"

"She left me . . ." Joe moaned. "For Iggy Pop." I was shocked, until Joe kicked me under the table and cracked up. We drank, laughed, and talked about life until six a.m. I was hurting pretty bad getting on the plane, but I didn't care. I was going back to England.

Ryan and I played beautiful theaters every night. Our first show was at the Royal Festival Hall in London. *Uncut*'s editor Allan Jones came by to say hello before I went on. So did the critic from the *Times*. I knew I had to live up to all that press—without my band or even a keyboard player.

To ease my nerves, I drank more than usual before I went on. I had so much adrenaline going that I didn't even feel it. I was really scared walking onto that wide, empty stage alone, facing an audience that had paid to see someone else. The silence was deafening.

But after the first song, the applause told me I had them. In between songs, I shared stories about my life as a van man, and getting arrested after playing Madison Square Garden. Hearing people laugh gave me courage. The audience responded to my set with warmth and enthusiasm, giving me a standing ovation. It was like nothing I'd ever experienced before. And it was like that every night for the rest of the tour.

After sound check, I would walk around town, looking for things I could work into my onstage bits. After the shows, we'd go out on the town. At a hotel bar in Stockholm, Ryan and I smashed a bunch of glasses and ran out, laughing our asses off. Then we tried this in another hotel, but a security guard grabbed Ryan and started punching him.

Sometimes I got homesick, and when I did, I called Howie. "Stop complaining," he'd say, "You're doing what you've always wanted to do, so enjoy it. This is what you dreamed about."

We'd have some laughs and I'd feel better. Howie always felt like home.

Chapter 31

Spray Paint Heroes

We never had a baby
But she got more tattoos
And I got more material for the blues
  —"Swinging Man"

The tour went great, but when I got back to New York I received some awful news: Joe Strummer had died three days before Christmas, at just fifty years old. Luce found him on the couch after he had taken the dogs for a walk in the woods near their home. I was heartbroken for her. Whenever you were around her and Joe, you could tell they were really in love.

Joe, it turned out, had an undiagnosed congenital heart defect. His big heart just gave out. Yes, he smoked, drank, and did a little blow—but he also ran marathons. When I was training for my first marathon, I asked him, "Did you quit smoking and drinking before the race?"

"Nah," he laughed, "you run so you can smoke and drink *more!*"

As the news spread, a people's shrine of bodega candles, flowers, photos, cards, and graffiti grew for days in front of Niagara—like the one in front of CBGB after Joey died.

A few weeks later, Diane called with happier news. Her former boss, Danny Goldberg, and his wife, Rosemary Carroll, had just listened to my album in his car—and they loved it. Danny had worked with everyone from Led Zeppelin to

Nirvana. He was a radical, curly haired New Yorker—like D Generation's old champion Daniel Glass. And guess what? Danny and Daniel were partners in a record label now.

In January 2003, *The Fine Art of Self-Destruction* came out on Artemis Records in the US. "When you make your next record, Jesse," Danny said, "please don't change the way you sing."

I went on tour with Counting Crows, then returned to Europe, with my band this time. At every show, audiences sang along to "Brooklyn" and all those other songs I had written in my crooked little apartment with my cats staring at me. The songs on *Fine Art* were arrows I had needed to shoot out to exes, friends, and foes. I never expected them to connect with strangers so far from home the way they did.

I loved our British tour manager, Brandon Knights, who was my age. We bonded over the U.K. Subs and old AC/DC, swapping childhood stories as we zoomed up and down the motorways, grabbing grub at Marks & Sparks like all the young dudes.

Sticca and Tony Rock'n'Rolla flew over to join this new pirate ship. Sticca broke Tony's balls constantly, bitching that he was loading the bus all wrong. Sticca said Tony was more excited about his dancing-Frankenstein tattoo than humping gear. Tony laughed off the jabs and pushed on through.

After the shows, I tried to take a page out of Strummer's book and connect with every single person who wanted to talk. We'd usually go straight from the merch table to a local bar, where we'd tell stories, do shots, and sing along to the jukebox until we got kicked out. Sure, sometimes I'd get trapped in a corner by some drunken punisher shouting the same story over and over again. But the people who come to the shows in their coolest clothes, and sing and dance their hearts out, deserve as much respect as those of us onstage—if not more.

I was single on this tour. Raff and I had gotten back together, but then we broke up again. I wasn't too worried; we always got back together.

I was meeting some interesting women, and having a little fun here and there. But most nights, I was content to return to my room alone and get some sleep. These shows were so satisfying in a way I had never felt before. I wasn't getting booed onstage, so I guess I didn't need to "win" offstage anymore.

In Copenhagen, I stopped to check my email at a grimy Internet shop with sticky keyboards—and was happy to see one from Raff. I opened it and read that she had fallen in love with a friend of mine. She raved about this guy and all the great sex they were having, really twisting the knife in deep. When I read that email I felt so low and alone, like I'd lost my last piece of home. I had pined for Jenny throughout my relationship with Raff, and she knew it. Now she was getting her revenge. I deserved it. But it hurt like hell—and I couldn't exactly run over to her apartment from Denmark and try to get her back.

Crazily enough, I heard that Jenny was on tour in England, playing bass with Speedball Baby. We met up in Manchester, where we spent a snowy night together and talked until dawn. It felt like a dream being with Jenny while I was singing about her onstage every night. But the same old question still hung in the air between us: could we ever make it work?

I envied friends back home who were getting married and having kids. I wanted a family, too—but right now I needed this life more. I loved being on the road. The long drives put me into a dreamy trance. Maybe it's the hypnotic rumble of the wheels, or watching the world pass by. Time is lost and my mind slips into strange places. Something about it makes me want to write. I started scribbling lyrics in my notebook for a new song, "Mona Lisa."

Steven's selling marijuana
Uptown to the prima donnas
Medicate the counterculture
9/11 baby boom

Steven Poss, my old pal and former Quintano's classmate, had lost his cushy A&R job at Sony Music. He was back living with his parents in Queens, dealing weed to get by. Lots of my friends in the music and nightlife businesses lost their jobs after 9/11, because New Yorkers were too scared to go out. They were shacked up inside watching TV and making babies.

Poss built a nice little business selling marijuana to his music-biz contacts. Art Garfunkel was one of his uptown clients. Garfunkel was very cautious; he made Poss meet him inside the same Central Park tunnel at the same exact time every week. I wish I had a photograph of that. "Last time I saw Garfunkel," Poss once told me, "he said, 'Me and my friend are getting back together.'" Paul Simon and Art Garfunkel famously despised each other, and hadn't spoken for at least a decade. But sure enough, Simon & Garfunkel soon reunited for a sold-out world tour. The dealer hears first, I guess.

Poss was still a little runt with a squeaky voice—maybe because he'd been smoking four packs of Marlboro Reds a day and drugging it up since he was eleven. Doctors gave him injections when he was a teenager to help him grow, but they never took.

I was always too scared to do drugs, but Poss and other

kids in the scene used to buy speed, angel dust, mescaline, and acid from the dealers roaming Washington Square Park. I'd be sitting next to Poss in class at Quintano's, and he'd start coughing up crazy colors.

Late one night, back when I was still a van man, Poss met me for drinks at King Tut's. "Jesse," he mumbled, after we'd had a few, "ya know that school we went to?" He twisted the silver Quintano's class ring on his finger. I never went back to get mine.

"Yeah?"

"That place was never accredited for college."

My mother was surely rolling in her grave, wishing she could climb out and shout, "I KNEW IT!"

"Who cares?" I shrugged. "It's four in the morning. We're bombed, we're wrecked. Our lives are ruined."

"You're right," Poss giggled.

The Fine Art of Self-Destruction sold more copies than all D Generation's records put together. I played a sold-out homecoming show at the Bowery Ballroom. As people say, New York is a great place to leave, but an even greater place to come back to.

After the show, I went out partying, even though I had bruised my ribs falling onstage and had to be in Toronto early the next morning for a TV show. I crawled onto the plane, and passed out cold on the flight north.

At the television studio, the crew was lighting me before we were about to go live.

"Jack!" I yelled.

Flanagan came over.

"Do I look like shit? Do I look totally burnt?"

"Yeah," Jack grinned. "You look totally burnt and you look like shit."

* * *

Josh Cheuse wanted to direct a music video for Joe Strummer's powerful cover of Bob Marley's "Redemption Song." But how do you make a video when your singer is dead?

On the Lower East Side, when someone beloved in the Latino community dies, a graffiti artist spray-paints a portrait on the wall of the bodega or bar where the person used to hang out. Josh asked graffiti artists Dr. Revolt and Zephyr to spray-paint Strummer's portrait onto Niagara's 7th Street wall for the video.

They started rattling their paint cans and spraying the wall before the sun came up. Josh filmed all day while Zephyr and Revolt painted. People from the neighborhood came by to lay down flowers and candles. So did friends of Joe's like Cinqué Lee, Jim Jarmusch, and Steve Buscemi. In true Strummer fashion, the shoot became a rowdy block party, as a crowd gathered to drink, smoke ganja, and dance into the night.

Joe's portrait was set against the colors of the Rasta flag: red, yellow, and green. It was kind of cartoonish, with Joe wearing big black sunglasses like some hipster Mr. Magoo. Beneath Joe, the artists painted, *Know Your Rights!* in big yellow letters. In the upper right corner, they added one of Joe's famous quotes: *The Future Is Unwritten.* I figured we'd paint over the mural once the shoot was done. But we left it up for a few days . . . and now, thousands of photos, postcards, and tattoos later, Joe is still there.

I thought that 9/11 would scare away a lot of people. The city would clear out and be more like it used to be. We would have real neighborhoods again, and affordable rent.

But instead, the opposite happened. America came to us big-time. More yuppies flooded into the East Village, shoving out the people who had made the neighborhood so beautiful and cool.

They didn't drive out the heroin, though.

Tony Rock'n'Rolla was Niagara's manager now. He was managing some good bands, too. But Tony was looking rough. He slumped around. He was late to work. The pupils of his blue eyes were as tiny as the head of a pin. Johnny T. and I were worried. We sat Tony down and gave him a warning.

"Tony," I said, "if you don't get it together, we're gonna have to fire you. And that sucks, 'cause you're my friend. You were the best—and now you're the worst." Tony started to cry. It killed me. I started to cry, too, but I pulled it back. Having to be the boss really sucks sometimes.

Tony got more fucked up, missing shifts or showing up barely able to function. We finally had to fire him, and Tony went home to his parents in Denver. I prayed he would get clean there.

About a year later, I came through Denver on tour. I called Tony and put him on the guest list for my show. He'd gotten his own apartment; I took that as a good sign. The band and I were staying at a Ramada Inn on Colfax Avenue nicknamed "the Rockmata." Let me tell you the cold facts of Colfax: It was rough, especially at night.

Tony missed the gig, but he showed up to the after-party at the hotel bar, strung out and carrying a brown paper bag. Inside was a glass jar with a fetus floating in formaldehyde. He tried to sell it to me for a thousand bucks.

"Who do you think I am, Howie Pyro?" I said. "I don't want that creepy thing!"

Tony wandered around the bar trying to sell it. It broke my heart to see him like that.

A few weeks later, I got a message that Tony had hanged himself in his closet. His parents were devastated. Everyone back in New York was sad as hell.

We threw a memorial for Tony at Niagara. His mother flew in, and entered a room packed with people who truly loved her son. We filmed Tony's friends telling stories about how he touched their lives, and gave his parents a copy of the video.

This was the first memorial at Niagara, but not the last. I'm glad I didn't know that evening how many more friends I would lose. In that little back room where we sang, danced, fought, and became friends for life, we would eventually raise our glasses to Giorgio, Poss, Todd Youth, Howie, Jae Monroe, Paul Cripple from Reagan Youth . . .

I act like nothing hurts
A bar becomes a church
A limousine a hearse
And you don't look back

Chapter 32

Broken Radio

I think I missed you my whole life
—"The Dreamers"

Harry Greenberger and I rumbled down a long dirt road in his car, with Anthrax guitarist Rob Caggiano in the backseat. Harry was my close friend and guitar tech. Rob was producing my third solo album, *Glitter in the Gutter*, for Green Day's label, Adeline Records.

Rob was an intense Italian American guy from the Bronx, with long black hair and a goatee. My bandmates and I called him "the Devil." He was determined to make a hit album that would boost me to stadiums. "A big record!" he shouted often, when we were in the studio. "Big!"

It was a gorgeous spring day in rural Colts Neck, New Jersey. We passed green pastures dotted with horses and acres of waving corn. The scene was almost absurdly bucolic, with weeping willows swaying in the warm breeze and birds darting around overhead.

"Whoa, look at that!" I cried, nudging Harry. Some peacocks were parading around in the grass by the side of the road.

"This has gotta be it," Harry muttered, turning into a gravel driveway. Stones crunched under our tires as we bumped along slowly. We reached a beautiful old farmhouse with a wide wooden veranda. Harry parked and we piled out. I snuck in a few quick stretches and deep breaths before we walked up to the house.

Toby Scott, the engineer on some of my favorite records, stood on the porch. He was in his late fifties, stocky and strong, with crinkly blue eyes and a cropped graying beard. Toby held the door open and we walked into the house. Inside was a state-of-the-art recording studio, with a Neve console and vintage microphones on stands. The walls were hung with old acoustic guitars, cowboy hats, Western blankets, and cow skulls.

We sat around chatting with Toby until we heard a motorcycle rattling up the gravel. In walked Bruce Springsteen, unbuckling his helmet. He was wearing motorcycle boots, beat-up jeans, and a blue T-shirt with the sleeves cut off.

"Hey Jess, how are you?" Bruce said, heading into the kitchen. "You want a beer or a banana or something?"

I asked for a glass of water. We sat at the kitchen table and Bruce asked me what I'd been up to, and how touring was going. Then we got up and went into the studio.

I guess I should explain how I wound up in Bruce Springsteen's home studio.

Five years earlier, when Diane and I were listening to final mixes for *The Fine Art of Self-Destruction* at Loho Studios, I said quietly, almost to myself, "I want Bruce Springsteen to hear this record." Diane and I looked at each other and burst out laughing, like, *Yeah, right!*

After *Fine Art* came out, I played the Light of Day benefit for Parkinson's disease at the Stone Pony in Asbury Park, New Jersey. I had contributed a cover of "Hungry Heart" to the *Light of Day* compilation album. I had chosen that tune because Joey told me that when he asked Bruce Springsteen to write a song for the Ramones, Bruce wrote "Hungry Heart." But Bruce's manager, Jon Landau, said, "Don't give it to them," and "Hungry Heart" became Bruce's first top ten hit.

I trotted into the Stone Pony's green room after my set, and there, to my surprise, was Bruce Springsteen, with his wife, Patti Scialfa, and Bob Gruen.

"I really like your version of 'Hungry Heart,'" Bruce said. "And I wanna hear your album, I've been reading great things about it."

"Wow, thanks!" I replied. "I'm glad you like it."

I motioned to Harry to for fuck's sake run to my merch table and grab a copy of *Fine Art* for Bruce. Bob took a few photos, and that was it.

A month later, Diane told me, "Bruce wants to call you."

Two weeks went by. No call. I figured it was all a joke. But the day after Thanksgiving, I woke up to a voicemail from Springsteen. I called him back right away.

"You just waking up?" he asked.

"Yeah," I chuckled.

"Ah, man, I miss those late-night hours. You have kids?"

"Nope, not yet."

"They're great, but they get you up early. I love the record, man. It reminds me of those Stones records from the early sixties. How'd you get that sound?"

I explained that we had recorded everything live in one room, with just three mics on the drums.

"I'm doing some holiday charity shows in Asbury," Bruce said. "Would you want to be in them?"

"Yeah, sure! I know lots of cool Christmas songs."

Bruce laughed. "No, I want to do *your* songs. My band's gonna back you."

Holy shit. I was stunned.

Diane drove me to Asbury Park for rehearsal. We were greeted by Bruce's assistant/bodyguard, Terry McGovern, a tough ex–Navy Seal who looked like Santa Claus on steroids.

I walked into a cavernous room with a full stage and lighting setup, including a teleprompter with my lyrics.

Bruce was wearing his Telecaster and a huge grin. He gave me a big hug and didn't give me a moment to get nervous. I plugged in my acoustic guitar, and we jumped right into playing "Queen of the Underworld," "Wendy," and "X-Mas." Bruce and I shared the vocal mic, and he sang harmony and played strong, driving rhythm guitar like the best sideman in the world.

I nearly missed our first show, though, because I let Trigger from Continental drive me to Asbury in his 1950s Buick. We wound up in a snowstorm with no heat or defroster. It took five hours to crawl south on those balding vintage tires. I was losing my mind. When Trigger finally pulled up to Convention Hall, I bolted from the car like a madman, slipping and sliding on the icy pavement in my high-top sneakers.

The moment I got backstage, Sticca grabbed me. "Bruce is looking for you! He keeps saying, 'Where's the kid? Where's the kid?'"

Sticca hustled me to the dressing room, where I was surrounded by legends. Danny DeVito, Jon Bon Jovi, Southside Johnny, Steve Van Zandt, and Sam Moore of the R&B group Sam & Dave were swapping stories and joking around. You could tell they'd known each other for decades. I was a tongue-tied outsider, happy to be in the room at all.

I fidgeted nervously, waiting for Bruce to call me up. When it was time, I stepped out of the dressing room and into the wings. I froze for a moment, realizing I was about to get up there with one the greatest live performers of our time. I was the new kid again. I flashed back to how scared I used to feel looking up at the school bus stairs as a scrawny little boy with an eye patch. I remembered my mother squeezing my hand. *Just get on the bus, Captain Hook.*

"I've got a new friend from New York City!" I heard Bruce shout. "He's got a new record out called *The Fine Art of Self-Destruction*. It's a *real* album. Every song on it is great. Let's give it up for Jesse Malin!"

We played together for three nights, and every performance was magic. After the last show, Bruce took everybody out to dinner at a fancy restaurant in Asbury, where we traded stories for hours. I didn't feel like the new kid anymore, and that was nice.

Bruce and I stayed in touch, sharing what we were listening to, and turning each other on to new records. Two years later, I went to see him play at the Tweeter Center in Boston. It was a great, festive show full of old American folk songs that he had given a new tough twist.

I went backstage and told Bruce, "I'm going to LA to make my next record. I might even move there. I need a change."

"If you want me to do anything," he said, "I'd love to be part of it."

I couldn't wait to tell Caggiano. I figured we'd ask Bruce to do something quick and easy, like play a guitar solo or sing a few harmonies. "No," Rob said, "he should sing on that song you wrote about your mom. You guys should do it as a duet."

"Broken Radio" was a very personal song for me. All my complicated feelings about losing my mother were wrapped up in it. At first, I couldn't imagine anyone else singing on it. But it was also about the magic and the power of hearing your favorite song come on the radio. Having one of radio's biggest voices sing it with me began to feel right.

I used to get so embarrassed, as a kid, when my mother sang along with the car radio. We might be sitting in traffic sweating our asses off because the air conditioner was broken, but if a song she loved came on, she would light up and burst out singing with this beautiful voice that I always forgot she had. My mother sang me and my sister to sleep sometimes when we were small. She'd sing "Somewhere Over the Rainbow" very quietly and sweetly, but with an underlying melancholia that made me feel sad, lying there in the dark. This may sound strange, but I would feel scared that she was going to leave me and my sister one day.

I mailed a demo of "Broken Radio" to Bruce's house in Colts Neck. I wrote out the lyrics with a Sharpie, and included a note: *This is a song about my mom, who died very young. She loved to sing along to the radio.* I didn't think anything would come of it, to be honest.

We were recording *Glitter in the Gutter* at Velvet Buddha Studios in Los Angeles, right behind the Circus Liquor neon clown that has been in lots of movies. I was staying in a fancy Hollywood apartment complex nearby. But whenever I went out for a walk, male drivers slowed and honked at me like I was back at the bus stop in Queens. If you walk in LA, people think you're a prostitute. *Buns Up on Santa Monica* was not the name of this album.

Rob was a tyrant in the studio. He made me sing every song a million times. I sang until my throat was raw; until my voice was burnt. "C'mon, let's do it again, Jesse. Sing it like you're singing to sixty thousand people! More energy! More! MORE!" I would get really fed up, but this was my shot. I didn't want to let down Rob, or my friends in Green Day who believed in me. I gave it my all, and then some.

Rob and his producing partner, Eddie Wohl—an equally intense hard-rock motherfucker—beat the crap out of my band, too. We put down hundreds of takes, but still Rob and Eddie roared, "MORE ENERGY! COME ON!!" until we were exhausted and battered. While we passed out on the studio couches, Rob and Eddie sat together at the mixing board, chuckling maniacally like Beavis and Butthead as they worked on the tracks.

I was struggling to maneuver my rental car out of the underground garage one afternoon, when my phone rang. It was Bruce. He said he really liked the song and would love to sing on it. "You wanna come out to the house?" he asked.

"That sounds cool," I said. Anything to get out of LA.

Rob and I flew into Newark, where Harry picked us up. After crashing at a hotel in my beloved Manhattan, we drove to Colts Neck the next morning.

So, that's how I wound up in Bruce Springsteen's home studio.

Bruce put on his headphones and Toby got him dialed in just right. Bruce sang the second verse of "Broken Radio," and all of the choruses. He gave us three beautiful takes. Hearing his warm, raspy voice on my song brought me chills. I had played *Nebraska* to comfort my mother on so many nights when she was dying and terrified. Now Bruce was singing the song I had written for her.

He took off his headphones. "What do you think, Jess?"

"It's great," I said. "It's very cool. I dig it."

Rob piped up: "Hey, Bruce, would you mind doing it just one more time?"

"Sure," Bruce said, putting on his headphones. He stepped up to the mic and sang all his parts again.

"Great! That was great!" Rob raved. "But could you do it again, one more time, with a little more energy?"

Bruce rubbed his goatee, but he sang through the entire song. Again.

Rob hit Bruce with his patented "Let's do it again! MORE ENERGY!" routine eight more times. I was mortified. I closed my eyes and prayed to become invisible so that I could fade into the walls.

I'll say this for the Devil: he is an equal-opportunity torturer. Bruce, though, is an extremely kind and humble guy. He put up with Rob and gave his all for every take.

Finally, Rob was satisfied, and I could breathe again.

Then Rob said, "Hey, Bruce, can you sing this line from the chorus—'*The angels love you more*'—just you alone at the end?"

Bruce sang the line with great emotion, adding the perfect touch to the song's haunting outro. Then he took off his headphones, stepped away from the mic, and turned to me. "Beautiful song, Jess."

And that was it.

I was so touched by Bruce's generosity, and the majesty he had added to "Broken Radio." We all hung out for a few minutes, and then Bruce rode his Harley into the woods. Harry and I looked at each other like, *Did this really just happen?* The whole experience was surreal.

My mother loved movies and musicals. She believed in Hollywood dreams. She would sing along with Frank Sinatra: "*Fairy tales can come true, it can happen to you, if you're young at heart.*"

I always wondered why she didn't really go for it, as a singer. I guess raising two kids as a single mom can sap your strength. But she never let on that times were tough. If she couldn't pay the electric bill and our lights went out, she just grabbed me and Juliet and took us to Carvel on Fourteenth Avenue for ice cream. Life was to be enjoyed, songs were to be sung, good things were right around the corner, and dreams could come true.

It could happen to you.

Epilogue

The Father, Son, and the Holy Ghost

My father had been left by his mother, my mother, and his second wife. He kept dating, running through girlfriends, trying to make it work. But he always had a backup waiting in the wings. When the music video for "Broken Radio" came out, he tried to show it to every unmarried woman in South Florida.

After he retired, we got a little closer. He even came to a couple of my shows. When he moved to Florida, I visited sometimes, but mostly I called him from airports and hotels on tour. He always wanted to know what I was working on. He liked Lucinda Williams and kept asking to hear some of the new record of mine that she was producing. He could be very critical, so I told him to wait until it was done. I wanted it to be right.

By then, my father was battling polycystic kidney disease. He got a kidney transplant and was in and out of hospitals. "If I die while you're out there, keep going," he would say. "The show must go on."

"American Pie" by Don McLean was one of my father's favorite songs of all time. He never got tired of telling me how he had to flip the single over on his turntable to hear the whole song, because it was so long. He told me the story many times about that fateful day when a small plane carrying Buddy Holly, the Big Bopper, and Ritchie Valens crashed in a snowy field. On tour, I found a poster for their final show at the Surf Ballroom in Clear Lake, Iowa. My father had it framed and hung it in his apartment.

The summer of 2017, I spent a lot of time with my dad in Florida hospitals. I was on tour in the UK when I got the call that he was going downhill fast. I grabbed a flight from London to JFK, with a connection straight to West Palm Beach, where Juliet was by his side. Right as I cleared US customs in JFK, I felt my phone ringing in my pocket. It was Juliet. She was crying. I think he held on until I was back home.

Near the end, my father had gotten it together with a wonderful woman—but he nearly screwed that up, too. After he died, I told her, "I'm amazed he was still driving only six weeks ago."

"Driving?" she laughed. "He was *cheating* on me just a month ago!"

She didn't leave him, she said, because she didn't want him to feel abandoned again, going into the next life.

They say to look for signs right after someone passes. I wasn't sure I believed in all that. A childhood friend of my father's gave me the address of the Bronx projects where they'd grown up. I took the 6 train up there one Sunday and walked around.

I sat on a bench outside his building, looking into the windows. The neighborhood was pretty run-down now. I probably didn't want to be there after dark. I strolled by his school and the baseball field where he had dreamed of joining the Yankees. I saw street signs with names I recognized from his stories. I got excited and wanted to tell him. Then I remembered I couldn't call him anymore.

I spotted a little health-food store and headed toward it. I've always found comfort wandering through these stores in strange towns, looking for stuff to eat on the road that won't kill me. Even this old neighborhood way up in the Bronx was gentrifying. I walked through the aisles in a daze. I turned a corner and heard music playing from a speaker on the ceiling. As I got closer, I caught my breath when I recognized the song. At that very moment, the last verse played:

> And the three men I admire most
> The Father, Son, and the Holy Ghost
> They caught the last train for the coast
> The day the music died

Nobody wants to see a fifty-year-old guy sobbing in a health-food store on a Sunday afternoon in the Bronx. I ran out as fast as I could. I stood under the elevated subway platform with the wind blowing hard and tears rolling down my face; I felt him there with me.

A week later, Juliet and I went to a Yankees game. During intermission, we snuck down to the edge of the stands with a bag of our father's ashes and threw them onto the field.

I started writing this book in my apartment in New York. I'm finishing it from a clinic in Buenos Aires, where I have been receiving stem-cell treatments for my spinal-cord injury and doing intensive physical therapy.

When I left New York, the doctors were not very optimistic. But now I can walk nearly a block on my own, with a walker. I can stand gripping a mic stand for one whole song wearing leg braces. Recently, I've given a few private performances for a small audience of family and friends, sitting down with my band. My voice is strong and I can still play guitar. Two things I'll never again take for granted.

These small victories have been hard-won. I am not giving up until I can walk onstage and give it all again.

Thanksgiving might be my favorite holiday. Every year, my friends come over for a stray-dog feast and we watch our favorite movies. This Thanksgiving, my old pal Jimmy G. surprised me by flying down to Buenos Aires. As we sat in my room, he pulled a ring from his pocket and handed it to me. Poss's silver graduation ring from Quintano's. I'm wearing it now.

They say when your parents die, you finally grow up.

I'd say I'm almost grown.

Jesse Malin
Buenos Aires

Thank you to:

Juliet Malin
Dave Bason
Debra Devi
Johnny Temple
Michael Imperioli